THE REASON OF THE GIFT

Richard Lectures for 2008

The Reason
of the Gift

JEAN-LUC MARION

Translated by Stephen E. Lewis

UNIVERSITY OF VIRGINIA PRESS

CHARLOTTESVILLE AND LONDON

University of Virginia Press
© 2011 by the Rector and Visitors of the
University of Virginia
All rights reserved

Printed in the United States of America on acid-free paper

First published 2011

1 3 5 7 9 8 6 4 2

LIBRARY OF CONGRESS CATALOGING-IN-PUBLICATION DATA
Marion, Jean-Luc, 1946–
[Lectures. English. Selections]
The reason of the gift / Jean-Luc Marion ;
translated by Stephen E. Lewis.
p.   cm. — (Richard lectures for 2008)
Includes bibliographical references (p.   ) and index.
ISBN 978-0-8139-3178-4 (cloth : alk. paper) —
ISBN 978-0-8139-3184-5 (e-book)
1. Phenomenology. I. Title.
B2430.M284A513 2011
194—dc22
2011015739

Contents

Translator's Acknowledgments

There are several people I would like to thank for their aid and encouragement as I worked on this project: John Crosby, Claude Romano, J. J. Sanford, and Paul Symington for helpful comments on the introduction; Jamie Kropka for his help preparing a first draft translation of chapter 1; Karl Hefty for sharing with me his translation of chapter 4; and Christina M. Gschwandtner for a careful reading of a complete draft of the translation. I also wish to express special thanks to the University of Virginia Press's anonymous reader, who offered many, many crucial suggestions for improvements to the entire translation. All mistakes that remain, of course, I acknowledge as mine. I dedicate this work to the memory of my mother-in-law, Judith Holm, † November 1, 2010.

The Phenomenological Concept of Givenness and the "Myth of the Given"

Stephen E. Lewis

The Reason of the Gift collects four essays that address the theme of givenness and the gift—central to Jean-Luc Marion's phenomenological project—through brilliant argumentation that is both historically informed and constructive. These essays thus exemplify characteristic aspects of Marion's way of doing philosophy. Three of the papers included in *The Reason of the Gift*—"The Phenomenological Origins of the Concept of Givenness," "Substitution and Solicitude: How Levinas Re-reads Heidegger," and "Sketch of a Phenomenological Concept of Sacrifice"—were delivered by Jean-Luc Marion as the James W. Richard Lectures at the University of Virginia, September 29–October 1, 2008. A fourth—"Remarks on the Origins of *Gegebenheit* in Heidegger's Thought"—was added for inclusion as the second essay in this volume.

The essays that make up *The Reason of the Gift* deepen the reader's sense of both the profundity and the range of engagement to be found in Marion's previous phenomenological work, and suggest for scholars at once the diversity and the richness of opportunities for exploration that surround the topics of givenness and the gift. In this introduction I shall sketch some of the ways in which we might see this book contributing to our understanding of Marion's phenomenological work, both past and present; then I shall focus on at least one way in which these essays contribute to the outline of what feels like an ever-more-necessary conversation between Marion's philosophical project and certain approaches to the topic of "the given" found in contemporary Anglo-American philosophy. In particular, I shall offer a suggestive exploration of what Marion's work might have to say to the account of givenness found in the "analytic Kantianism" of John McDowell, as it has developed out of Wilfrid Sellars's account of the "Myth of the Given" and, even more fundamentally, out of the neo-Kantian debate with empiricism that forms the background to the historical investigations Marion carries out in the first two essays in this book.[1]

The four essays collected in *The Reason of the Gift* provide significant historical context for Marion's phenomenology of givenness while at the same time extending its constructive reach. The first two essays chart genealogies for the concept of givenness as it was adopted and adapted for the purposes of nonobjective (or nonobjectivizing) thought by Husserl and Heidegger, respectively, from its role in the various theories of the object developed by Bernard Bolzano, Alexius Meinong, Heinrich Rickert, Paul Natorp, and Emil Lask. These genealogies offer valuable supplementary insights into the principal development of Marion's phenomenological project as it emerges out of the predominantly historical 1989 study of Husserl and Heidegger, *Réduction et donation: Recherches sur Husserl, Heidegger et la phénoménologie*, and the predominantly constructive work in phenomenological method entitled *Étant donné: Essai d'une phénoménologie de la donation*, published in 1997.[2] In these books, the story Marion tells about givenness centers on the use of the phenomenological reduction and the extent to which different degrees of reduction allow the full phenomenality of the phenomenon to appear, according to the principle "So much reduction, so much givenness." While Husserl and Heidegger both "have recourse to givenness and espouse its function as ultimate principle" (*ED* 59/ *BG* 38), they each, according to Marion, in different ways fail to radicalize adequately the reduction so that it leads phenomena all the way back to originary givenness, or, as Kevin Hart has put it, "to the originary giving intuition [*originär gebende Anschauung*]—

that is, the *self*-givenness [*Selbstgegebenheit*]—of phenomena."[3] This reduction to givenness is philosophically crucial because, as Hart explains, "[o]nly then will one secure experience as *Evidenz*, evidence or, better, self-evidence: the direct awareness of phenomena as they manifest themselves."[4] Husserl, says Marion, reduces the phenomenon to its objectity, its status as object of consciousness, while Heidegger reduces the phenomenon to beingness, its status as a being or entity within the horizon of Being. In each case, says Marion, these reductions place "conditions and determinations" on phenomena, stopping them short of a reduction all the way to their originary (unconditioned) givenness (*RD* 305/*RG* 205).

A phenomenon that exceeds and precedes the horizons of objectivity and being—what Marion calls a "saturated phenomenon"—also necessarily exceeds and precedes the thinking "I" that sets up and employs these horizons. Thus, integral to Marion's understanding of phenomena as given is his understanding of the I affected by the given as called forth, or given birth to, in the very givenness of that which gives. This I receives herself from what she receives (*ED* 366/*BG* 266); she is the "witness constituted by what gives itself."[5] Indeed, the I that correlates to the reduction to givenness—what Marion in *Being Given* names the *adonné*, the one literally given over to or gifted by/in givenness—is "by nature" the I who is, literally, born.[6] For birth, as Marion suggests in *In Excess* and shows in greater detail in his 2010 book *Certitudes négatives*, is the event that makes us ever latecomers to that which has already been happening. The experience of birth discloses "the *event-hood* [*l'événementialité*] that sustains and sets off every phenomenon as an event that happens [*se* passe]" (*CN* 298).[7] To experience reality as the natural-born I—also called by Marion the witness, or the gifted (the *adonné*)—is to experience phenomena that, without any engineering on our part, happen in their own right, giving themselves to us—as opposed to phenomena as objects that we constitute from a position of spectatorial priority (*CN* 298).[8] Put in terms of knowledge—of the attempt to develop concepts to match intuitions—the witness plays his part in the interval between, on the one hand, the indisputable and incontestable excess of intuition lived and, on the other, the never compensated lack of the concepts that would render this experience an objective experience—in other words, that would make it an object. The witness, who knows what he saw and that he saw it, does not comprehend it by one or more adequate concepts. As a result, he undergoes an affection of the event and remains forever late to it. Never will he (re-)constitute it [. . .].[9]

The witness thus distinguishes himself

> from the engineer, the inventor or the "conceiver" [*concepteur*—the French word used for a designer, e.g., a website designer, a lighting designer] who produces objects because he comprehends them in terms of their concept before turning to any actual intuition, indeed without recourse to it at all. And in *this* sense, it could be said that the "conceiver," in contrast to the witness, accomplishes the "creation of events." This oxymoron becomes thinkable only as the denegation of the saturated phenomenon by the power of technology, which attempts to produce objects even there where the event unrolls.[10]

In *The Reason of the Gift*, the first two essays, which trace the securing of *Gegebenheit* for phenomenology from its entanglement with objective thinking in neo-Kantianism, make clear in even more detail than heretofore in Marion's work the path of a nonobjectifying philosophy that Marion's project travels. For readers of Marion in English, these two essays establish a background in the history of philosophy for Marion's subsequent emphasis and analytical focus—both in his response to critics of the concept of saturated phenomena ("The Banality of Saturation") and in his recent effort to introduce the concept of a "negative certitude" into philosophy (*Certitudes négatives*)—on nonobjective experience, or what he feels is better referred to as "counter-experience."[11]

I would like to turn now to a historically informed comparison of the respective approaches to "the given" and "givenness" in Marion, on the one hand, and Sellars and McDowell on the other. My focus will be on Sellars's famous account of the "Myth of the Given" as it appears in his lengthy essay "Empiricism and the Philosophy of Mind," and on McDowell's elaboration of the issues surrounding the Myth of the Given in his book *Mind and World*.[12]

Indeed, for some time now, readers of Marion have called for just such a comparison.[13] In *Being Given*, Marion himself sketches what amounts to an outline for the comparison when, after claiming that "every phenomenon falls within the given, to the point that the terms [phenomenon and given] could trade places," he writes that "phenomenology agrees with empiricism in privileging recourse to the fact, even if it stands apart from it in refusing to limit the facts solely to sensible empiricity" (*BG* 119/ *ED* 169, trans. modified). For Marion there is, then, an important distinction to draw between the way empiricism privileges facts—by limiting its focus to their "sensible empiricity"—and the way phenomenology does so. This rather offhand point is elaborated a bit—though in a fairly cursory manner, it is true—in *The Reason of the Gift*. Readers will notice at the very beginning of the book's first essay ("The Phenomenological Origins of the Concept of Givenness") that Marion quickly seeks to dispel any hasty connection one might draw between *Gegebenheit* as it figures in phenomenology and "the given" as it figures in various other philosophical approaches, including different moments in the history of empiricism. It is not, he writes, a matter here of

taking up once again—doubtless one time too many—the debate over the possibility of unconstituted givens, whether they be understood in the manner of sense data, as in the Lockean tradition; or as the contents of *Erlebnisse* in the debate concerning protocol statements between Carnap and Neurath; or, in the Bergsonian style, as immediate givens of consciousness. For the principle—supposing that there is one—that everything that shows itself must first give itself (even if everything that gives itself nevertheless does not show itself completely) implies that one is questioning given-ness as *a mode of phenomenality*, as the *how* or *manner (Wie)* of the phenomenon. So that the issue is no longer the imme-diate given, the perceptive content, or the lived experience of consciousness—in short, of something that is given *(das Gegebene)*, but instead of the style of its phenomenalization *insofar as* it is given, which is to say, the issue is its *given-ness (Gegebenheit)*. [. . .] Thus the terrain of the debate, as well as its stake, found itself shifted from the theory of knowledge *(Erkenntnistheorie)* to phenomenality, and thus to phenom-enology. *(The Reason of the Gift,* 19, 20)

In this paragraph, Marion quickly names three modern philo-sophical traditions that, according to their particular approaches, speak of the given in ways that are to be clearly distinguished from the ways in which givenness is used in phenomenology to describe the "*how* or *manner* [. . .] of the phenomenon." The first two approaches that Marion mentions—those conceiving of the given as unconstituted, whether in terms of sense-data or protocol statements—are stigmatized by Sellars under his head-ing "the Myth of the Given" as illegitimate attempts to ground knowledge in a pre- or nonconceptual foundation. But Sellars believes that his critique of the given goes beyond this empiri-cist foundationalism to implicate *givenness* as well: "If [. . .] I begin my argument with an attack on sense-datum theories, it is only as a first step in a general critique of the entire framework of givenness" (EPM 128). Our question, then, becomes: Does givenness in phenomenology—as the "*how* or *manner* [. . .] of the phenomenon"—somehow escape or avoid the condemnation of Sellars and those working in his wake, such as McDowell? And how does Marion's discussion of the emergence of the phenom-enological understanding of givenness out of the neo-Kantian *Erkenntnistheorie* contribute, if at all, to our understanding of the relationship of phenomenological givenness in Marion to "the Myth of the Given" in Sellars and McDowell?

I will try to answer these questions in two ways: historically and, briefly and in a cursory way, constructively. A historical answer can proceed by linking Marion's accounts of Husserl's and Heidegger's respective efforts to wrest *Gegebenheit* free from the objectifying clutches of neo-Kantianism with an account, recently provided by Claude Romano in his book *Au coeur de la raison, la phénoménologie* (2010), of the implication of Sellars's and McDowell's approach to the given and givenness within the same neo-Kantian objectifying approach to the given.[14] As for the constructive answer: once we have appreciated the historical dimensions of the arguments about the given and givenness in the thought of Marion and of Sellars and McDowell, we will consider how an awareness of the difference between the two conceptions of the given and givenness can help us to better understand some of the critical questions that still surround Marion's concept of the saturated phenomenon.

As we have already noted, the first half of *The Reason of the Gift* tells the story of the emergence of a phenomenological understanding of givenness from the debates in which the early Heidegger and the late Husserl engaged with the theory of the object in Bolzano, Meinong, and the neo-Kantianism of Natorp and Rickert. Here I will simply note the main points that Marion makes in his account of this moment in the history of philosophy, and connect these with Romano's account. This will then prepare us to discuss Romano's argument that Sellars and McDowell essentially repeat, apparently without realizing it, a neo-Kantian debate with empiricism from which phenomenology extricated itself early in the twentieth century.

This extrication is the primary focus of Marion's two essays on the emergence of givenness as a phenomenological concept in *The Reason of the Gift*. A quotation from Heidegger's 1919 course, one of the central texts considered by Marion in "Remarks on the Origins of *Gegebenheit* in Heidegger's Thought," allows Marion to focus his history on two philosophical currents that Heidegger sees implicated by the "problem of givenness," namely, a two-variety neo-Kantian "philosophy as the knowledge of things," on the one hand, and phenomenology, on the other, characterized here as "philosophy as the entry way into the experience of the world" (*The Reason of the Gift*, 36). Heidegger states: "The problem of givenness is not a particular [and] specific problem. With it, the paths of the modern doctrines of knowledge diverge from one another and, at the same time, [they diverge] from phenomenology, which must first deliver the problem from a constricted problematic of epistemology."[15] In this essay, then, Marion shows how the early Heidegger seeks to "deliver" phenomena (such as the memorable example of the professor's lectern) from neo-Kantian thingification or objectification,[16] in order that they instead may appear given out of an environment *(Umwelt)* rich with the signification within which they abide (see *The Reason of the Gift*, 46–48).

The story told in "The Phenomenological Origins of the Concept of Givenness" fills out and expands this history of the "problem of givenness," demonstrating across a broad array of contemporaries of Husserl and Heidegger the way in which the concept of givenness can be seen to come to open "a gap [. . .] between being and objects," such that "by saying *es gibt* where one cannot say *it is*, this gap allows for a step back [*Schritt zurück*], outside of being, and perhaps outside of metaphysics as well" (*The Reason of the Gift*, 32).

Thus acquainted with Marion's account in *The Reason of the Gift* of phenomenology's extrication of the concept of givenness from thingification and objectification, we can turn to a chapter of Romano's study, which expands the historical context of the problem of givenness by discussing the debate between Marburg school neo-Kantianism and contemporary empiricism, out of which there comes precisely those conceptions of givenness in Natorp and Rickert that Heidegger then responded to critically in the texts that Marion explores. Romano argues for the importance of recognizing how the neo-Kantian conception of givenness emerges out of debate with classical empiricism because, he says, present-day discussions of whether or not experience contains nonconceptual content are weak or lacking in sophistication and insight exactly owing to the lack of awareness they betray of the history of this debate, and the important role that phenomenology played in shifting the debate in productive ways.[17]

We are seeking to arrive at a point where we can get a clear view of the upshot of the confrontation between phenomenology, which claims that experience contains non- (including pre-) conceptual material, and the analytic Kantianism of Sellars and McDowell, which claims, in the words of McDowell, that "conceptual capacities are already operative in the deliverances of sensibility themselves" (*MW* 39), and that "capacities of spontaneity [conceptual capacities] [. . . are] in play all the way out to the ultimate grounds of empirical judgements" (*MW* 67). In order to arrive at this confrontation, it will be useful to summarize the main points of Romano's account.

Romano's story begins at the outset of the twentieth century, when three major currents occupied the philosophical stage: the inheritors of classical empiricism (Romano mentions Mach), the neo-Kantians (Romano tends to use Natorp as the primary representative of the Marburg school), and the phenomenologists (principally Husserl and Heidegger). The neo-Kantians opposed themselves to the classical empiricists but, points out Romano, shared with them the same framework of thought regarding the conceptualization of the given:

> Instead of admitting an immediate given that would be the starting point of all knowledge [like the empiricists], [the neo-Kantians] consider this given as already mediated by concepts, put into form by conceptual schemata or symbolic forms that necessarily involve language. More precisely, in critiquing the given of the empiricists, they end up by rejecting the idea of the given *in general*—and they reject it because they continue to conceive of every given, after the fashion of their empiricist adversaries, as devoid of immanent meaning and structuring. They thus refuse the Kantian idea of the two sources of human knowledge (sensibility and understanding, receptivity and spontaneity); they affirm that experience receives "from on high" its meaning and its

structuring, thanks to the "logical" functions of thought, of science, and of culture. By refusing the title of knowledge to the given and instead assigning all knowledge to the sphere of judgment, they diametrically oppose facts and values, causality and justification. (728–29)

For Romano's story, this decision on the part of the neo-Kantians to adopt, even in their refusal, the very same way of conceiving of the given as that held by their adversaries the classical empiricists carries over—seemingly unwittingly—into the analytical Kantianism (what Romano simply terms "néokantisme analytique") of Sellars and McDowell.[18] Like the neo-Kantians, Sellars and McDowell maintain that the given is necessarily "devoid of immanent meaning and structure"—phenomena do not appear, like Heidegger's example of the lectern, as given out of an environing world rich in signification. Experience, too, is entirely conceptual, through and through, "all the way out," as McDowell puts it (*MW* 67)—or, as Sellars puts it in a characteristic passage from "Empiricism and the Philosophy of Mind," "the ability to recognize that something *looks* green, presupposes the concept of *being green*, and [. . .] the latter concept involves the ability to tell what colours objects have by looking at them—which, in turn, involves knowing in what circumstances to place an object if one wishes to ascertain its colour by looking at it" (EPM 146). There is no such thing as a nonconceptual or even preconceptual perception or intuition, and the always already conceptual structure of intuitions is understood to be "a linguistic affair" (EPM 160). Sellars makes this clear when he states that the knowledge of the "circumstances [in which] to place an object if one wishes to ascertain its colour by looking at it" are the conditions "in which colour words have their primary perceptual use" (EPM 147n1). Discourse and discursive thought, then, are integral to perceptual knowledge for Sellars and McDowell.

Regarding this understanding of conceptual thought as essentially linguistic, Romano makes the case for the importance of Ernst Cassirer's *Philosophy of Symbolic Forms* as the link between

Marburg school neo-Kantianism and early analytic philosophy; for Cassirer, writes Romano, "the spontaneity of the mind [— its conceptual capacity—] is attested in symbolic forms, starting from the very level of what one wrongly terms 'intuition'" (739). We have already touched upon the difference between the phenomenological concept of givenness and the neo-Kantian account of the given, as explored in *The Reason of the Gift*; let us now move toward a characterization of the difference between the phenomenological concept of givenness and the account of the given in Sellars and McDowell, based on Romano's historical argument. According to Romano, phenomenology evades the "Myth of the Given" because its concepts do not fit "into the coordinates of the empiricism/Kantianism debate," especially the epistemological problematic that is central to that debate (730). As Marion's essays in *The Reason of the Gift* on the phenomenological concept of givenness make clear, phenomenology rejects the subject-object framework that, in Romano's words, "aims to show how experience is put into form from the exterior, by conceptual schemata" (730). Phenomenology, he writes, does not claim

to derive thought from experience, as empiricism would have it, or, on the contrary, to derive the order that governs experience from the order that governs thought [. . .]. [Instead, phenomenology] postulates that experience is already reasonable [*sensée*] and structured before the intervention of discursive language and thought, that it possesses its own proper order and an immanent articulation, and is in no case reduced to the naked reception of a "given" such as is recognized by empiricism and only *partially* criticized by Kantianism. Instead of criticizing the very notion of the given, and conferring upon it a mythological status under the pretext that such a given would always already be informed by concepts and categories, [phenomenology] strives to broaden the concept of the given itself well beyond *sense-data*, in order to think an *experience* of the world, but also of art, of culture, of human interactions and institutions, of history, and even of language. [. . .] Phenomenology thus refuses to follow in the footsteps of the neo-Kantian critique of the given, which, in its eyes, bears only upon an atrophied concept of the given, and in no way upon experience in its comprehensive meaning, which phenomenology is concerned to promote. (730–31)[19]

Romano's historically based claim that Sellars and McDowell are essentially the second and third acts, respectively, in a nearly century-long neo-Kantian debate with empiricism[20] may be useful in efforts to evaluate the reach and persuasiveness of certain objections to Marion's concepts of the saturated phenomenon and the gifted (the *adonné*). Two examples of what I mean can be quickly and suggestively sketched. As suggestive sketches, they make no claim to a thoroughgoing evaluation of the critiques in question. But I do feel that they make evident the potential constructive value of the historical lessons that Marion and Romano each offer.

The first suggestive sketch seeks to evaluate from the point of view of the Marion-Sellars-McDowell comparison the critique made by Marlène Zarader of Marion's attempts to introduce the saturated phenomenon and the *adonné* into phenomenology. She expresses her doubts about Marion's project by suggesting that it is, in fact, logically impossible as a *phenomenological* project. She writes that "it is indeed possible to think without contradiction an experience without object, but [. . .] the same is not true for an experience without subject[; . . .] givenness [cannot be] sever[ed] [. . .] from any constituting pole[:] that is the prohibition that one cannot breach without seeing the very ground of phenomenology slip away."[21] She concludes her essay with a statement about the proper conceptualization of the given—in the terms of her essay, the given as the transcendent—which figures the given as a ghostly, mythic dream that contains "everything that disturbs [an] immanence" made up only of the objects, beings, and subjects that are able to appear in phenomenality (117). Zarader writes,

THE REASON OF THE GIFT

What, then, is the given? Nothing but immanence, nothing but a fragile, precarious, ever-threatened immanence. To think without contradiction the "and" in the copula "phenomenality and transcendence" presupposes abandoning all hope of a pure revelation of the transcendent in the phenomenal, in favor of an approach concerned with phenomenality's entry into crisis, with no outside discernible other than this crisis itself. And it is within this internal trembling of immanence that the possibility of transcendence remains as a hollow inscription—a transcendence that can function only, in phenomenological discourse, as a *critical*, and never positive, possibility. (118)

When Zarader, speaking from within phenomenology, is read alongside McDowell, some interesting parallels appear. The primary difference between the two critiques of the given seems primarily (and merely) one of mood toward the mythic. Where McDowell finds therapeutic "escape" from "intolerable" philosophical anxiety[22] in the elimination of the mythical given through the thought that "the conceptual is unbounded" (*MW* 44), Zarader's description of a homologous elimination of the given, this time by immanent phenomenality, results in a melancholy, yet "critical" feeling. For Zarader, the given as transcendence is abandoned as a logical impossibility, and phenomenality, now necessarily immanent, enters into a "crisis, with no outside discernible," "trembling" at the haunting disturbance caused by the "*critical*, and never positive, possibility" of the given. McDowell eliminates the mythical given with a satisfied sense of relief; Zarader does so with a sense of guilt.[23]

The second example meant to show the usefulness of an awareness of the neo-Kantian critique of the given when evaluating the persuasiveness of critical attacks on Marion's concept of givenness and saturated phenomena engages with a passage in Shane Mackinlay's recent book *Interpreting Excess: Jean-Luc Marion, Saturated Phenomena, and Hermeneutics*. The book argues, carefully and with nuance, that Marion insufficiently recognizes the active, essentially hermeneutic activity that is required in any human reception of phenomenality. As a result of this failed recognition, says Mackinlay, Marion wrongly and impossibly absolutizes the givenness of saturated phenomena, and likewise wrongly insists upon the possibility of human passivity in front of such phenomena. In the passage I've chosen to focus on here, Mackinlay charges Marion with having contradicted himself by at one point in his body of work insisting that the failure to appreciate phenomena as saturated results from their incorrect theoretical description (associated with Kant), only later to argue that saturated phenomena appear as unsaturated or "poor" phenomena when they are incorrectly approached and encountered. Mackinlay formulates this contradiction at one point with the following question, which he then sets about to answer: "If saturated phenomena are only able to appear as saturated when we *refrain* from reducing them to objects, does our *allowing* them to appear as saturated compromise their initiative and independence in showing themselves, and perhaps even result in a form of constitution?" (108–9). Mackinlay's answer to this question is of course in the negative, because he believes that the contradiction can only be resolved when we admit that "an actively receptive stance that is prior to the appearance of phenomena" is always in play (175). To illustrate why the presumption of this actively receptive stance prior to the appearance of phenomena is superior to Marion's seemingly contradictory position, which claims both that saturated phenomena *must* appear *of themselves* in order to appear as such, and that we can *allow* them to so appear, Mackinlay imagines two observers of a red car who nevertheless see the phenomenon differently. Mackinlay writes,

> The issue here is about the accurate recognition of phenomena, instead of the restriction of their appearing. [. . . T]he problems [. . .] arise from the idea of a phenomenon appearing as itself but being seen as something else. Given that a phenomenon *is* an appearance, if it is *seen as* something else, in what sense could it still *appear as* itself?
> The particular difficulty in this alternative interpretation

can be illustrated by considering a person who is color-blind. If a car appears red to one observer but green to another observer who is color-blind, this does not mean that a red *appearance* appears as green to the color-blind observer. While the car may indeed *be* red (in a nonphenomenal sense), there is no sense in which it *appears* as red to the color-blind observer. For the first observer, the (red) car appears red, while for the color-blind observer the same car appears green. There is no intermediate stage (of red appearing) added into the phenomenon's appearing (as green) for the color-blind observer; the car simply appears green for him, just as it appears red for the first observer. In the same way, if Marion's critique of Kant is interpreted as an accusation of "saturation-blindness," then what appears to the Kantian observer is simply an object rather than a saturated phenomenon that is appearing as an object due to inaccurate recognition. Because phenomena must appear (by definition), a saturated phenomenon cannot appear as an (unsaturated) object and still be a saturated *phenomenon*. In this case, the saturated phenomenon would not *actually* appear at all, and would only be a *potentially* saturated phenomenon, just as above, with its appearing dependent upon the perceiver. (111)

In this example, Mackinlay seeks to eliminate the possibility of willful blindness to the reception of saturated phenomena, and as a result he in many respects converts the hermeneutic issue involved in recognizing a phenomenon as saturated into the sort of epistemological problem that Sellars and McDowell for their part solve with "the myth of the given" and its associated positions on concepts and perception. Indeed, I find Mackinlay's staging of comparative appearances or looks[24] in this illustration to be highly reminiscent of Wilfrid Sellars's account in "Empiricism and the Philosophy of Mind" of John the tie salesman and his efforts to learn how a tie "looks" under different lighting conditions. As John "becomes more and more sophisticated about his own and other people's visual experiences," writes Sellars, "he learns under what conditions it is as though one were seeing a

necktie to be of one colour when in fact it is of another. [. . .]
And [. . .] *which* conditions are standard for a given mode of perception is, at the common sense level, specified by a list of conditions which exhibit the vagueness and open texture characteristic
of ordinary discourse" (EPM 147). Because according to Sellars's
"psychological nominalism," "*all* awareness of *sorts, resemblances,
facts,* etc., in short, all awareness of abstract entities—indeed, all
awareness even of particulars—is a linguistic affair," the fact that
in Mackinlay's example one observer is color-blind and another
is not presents no difficulties for the deployment of Sellarsian
logic there (EPM 160). Both observers of the red car, once they
have "purged" their "sensations and images [. . .] of epistemic
aboutness," will discover that "the primary reason for supposing that the fundamental associative tie between language and
the world must be between words and 'immediate experiences'
has disappeared, and [that] the way is clear to recognizing that
basic word-world associations hold, for example, between 'red'
and red *physical objects,* rather than between 'red' and a supposed
class of private red particulars" (EPM 161).

The apparent ease with which Sellars's account of the conceptual (discursive) makeup of perceptual awareness can be seen
operating in Mackinlay's critique here of a particular aspect of
Marion's account of saturated phenomena leads one to suspect
that Mackinlay has momentarily lost sight of the breadth that
characterizes the phenomenological concept of givenness, and
has instead narrowed the issues surrounding the reception of
saturated phenomena to an epistemological problematic of perception. Anthony J. Steinbock helpfully reminds us of the decisive aspects of looking that are essential to the reception of phenomena, and which have been stripped out in the example of the
appearance of the red car. Foremost among them is the erotic
aspect:

> Someone who does not dispose himself or herself, who has
> not made an "immanent decision," will not see the given.
> The poor phenomenon, in the sense of the denigrated phe-

nomenon, is what I see without wanting to see. I see in ordinary terms without receiving; I "merely" constitute it. I master it before I could receive it or "want" to receive it. The problem is not on the "side" of phenomenal givenness, but on the side of the "subject," a subject who has to be understood more fundamentally as the gifted.[25]

Steinbock goes on to point out that, for Marion, this lack of decisiveness in front of phenomenal givenness can arise either from the gifted's "essential finitude" (*ED* 425/*BG* 309), or from his or her unwillingness to decide for the gift (*ED* 426/*BG* 310)—there is both the "'can/could' of receiving and the 'want/would' of receiving."[26] Thus, here, too, color-blindness is not an impediment to the seeing of saturated phenomena, but for a different reason than for Sellars and, at least in the passage I have focused upon, for Mackinlay: deeper than the epistemological problematic involved is the question of the gifted's affection for what appears.[27]

The important place of affection, or love, in Marion's conception of givenness and, particularly, in his description of the nonreciprocal reason that governs the reception and the giving of gifts could lead us into discussion of the third and fourth essays included in *The Reason of the Gift*—"Substitution and Solicitude: How Levinas Re-reads Heidegger" and "Sketch of a Phenomenological Concept of Sacrifice." But space and the focus of this introduction foreclose that possibility. It will have to be enough here to conclude by suggesting that the rationality which makes *The Reason of the Gift* cohere as a book involves human affection for the fact that "it gives" in the diverse manifold of human experience.

ONE

The Phenomenological Origins
of the Concept of Givenness

I

In recent debates, especially within the French-speaking world, we have seen a question reappear that one might have thought definitively settled after the stubborn refutations of what was qualified (or rather disqualified) under the title of the "myth of the given"—the question, precisely, of *Gegebenheit.* Yet it was not a matter of taking up once again—doubtless one time too many—the debate over the possibility of unconstituted givens, whether they be understood in the manner of sense-data, as in the Lockean tradition; or as the contents of *Erlebnisse* in the debate concerning protocol statements between Carnap and Neurath; or, in the Bergsonian style, as immediate givens of consciousness. Rather, the point was to question the mode of being, or, better, of manifestation (precisely *not* the mode of *being*) of certain phenomena. For the principle—supposing that it be one—that everything that shows itself must first give itself (even if everything that gives itself nevertheless does not show itself without remainder)[1] implies that one is questioning givenness as *a mode of phenomenality,* as the *how* or *manner (Wie)* of the phenomenon. The issue, then, is no longer the immediate given, the perceptive content, or the lived experience of consciousness—in short, of something that is given *(das Gegebene),* but instead of the style of its phenomenalization *insofar as* it is given, or in short, its *givenness (donnéité) (Gegebenheit).*[2] The sometimes suspected ambiguity of the French word *donation* is in fact limited, for *donation* reflects the ambiguity of the German *Gegebenheit*, which indicates both that which finds itself given *(das, daß)* and its mode of manifestation *(Wie)*. Thus the place of the debate, as well as its stake, found itself shifted from the theory of knowledge *(Erkenntnistheorie)* to phenomenality, and thus to phenomenology. But this shift itself promptly opened up another question: is givenness *(donation)* limited and able to stand on its own supposed phenomenological determination—that of given-ness *(donnéité)*, of *Gegebenheit* in the sense of a mode of phenomenality—or does it inevitably slide toward givenness as an ontic process? One could thus understand givenness as a gift (in the more general framework of a sociology of the gift), as a modality of production (according to economy or technology), or indeed as a substitute for creation (in the theological sense, here generalized or tacit). It was sometimes this last hypothesis that was privileged, out of suspicion that in givenness lay the simple restoration, hidden but easily spotted, of creation, itself understood in the purely onto-theological sense as a transcendent causality and grounding.[3]

My intention in this essay will only be to verify the strictly phenomenological status of givenness, and therefore to understand it as a mode of phenomenality and not as an ontic given—as a *given-ness (Gegebenheit)*, and not as a metaphysical and onto-theological foundation. This verification can be conceived of in two ways: either by a strictly conceptual analysis, which would trace back from the crisis of every *a priori* foundation toward the necessary recourse to an *a posteriori* principle, as paradoxical as this formulation might at first seem—this is something I have attempted elsewhere.[4] Or—and this more modest path is the one we will follow here—by sketching the phenomenological genealogy of the concept of givenness or *Gegebenheit*, as found in certain uses in the early Heidegger and in late Husserl, respectively, as they worked with the theory of the object, such as it was developed by Bolzano, Meinong, and their contemporaries.

II

To establish the phenomenological status of givenness beginning with Heidegger, we could proceed, without any transition, to *Zeit und Sein*, which develops quite explicitly the original function of *es gibt*. Nevertheless, I shall not take this route, because, in a certain way, this text, more aporetic than it is conclusive, does not establish givenness in detail, but instead supposes it as already secured: the thesis that *es gibt Sein*, *es gibt Zeit* serves as point of departure, without ever being granted a genuine phenomenological exposition. And this starting point itself remains rather provisional, since the double *es gibt* ends up by quickly canceling itself in the *Ereignis*, the anchoring of which in *Gegebenheit* soon becomes quite problematic.[5] Instead, then, we might reverse course and take up one of the texts from the very beginning—specifically, the very first course from Freiburg, taught during the *Kriegsnotsemester* of 1919. But this approach remains debatable: even if the discussion Heidegger was then conducting with Natorp and Rickert opened up the right perspective (which I will confirm here), the young Heidegger did not yet have at his disposal the analytic of *Dasein*, or even the hermeneutics of facticity, with the result that these shortcomings color with a considerable indecision his moreover frequent uses of *es gibt*, *Gegebenheit*, and even *Ereignis*.[6] The risk of drawing incorrect correspondences in this reading between the beginning and the eventual accomplishment, and of making imprudent anticipations, would become almost inevitable. It seems, then, that the surest path is to examine the function and the reach of givenness in *Sein und Zeit* itself; for even if these do not affect the occurrences of *Gegebenheit*,[7] but of *es gibt*, they appear as significant as they are difficult to interpret.

Let us note first of all that, from the moment the formal position on the question of being is articulated (at §2), the first occurrence of the expression *es gibt* arises: "Aber 'seiend' nennen wir vieles und in verschiedenem Sinne. Seiend ist alles, wovon wir reden, was wir meinen, wozu wir uns so und so verhalten, seiend ist auch, was und wie wir selbst sind. Sein liegt im Daß- und Sosein, in Realität, Vorhandenheit, Bestand, Geltung, Dasein, im 'es gibt.' An *welchem* Seienden soll der Sinn von Sein abgelesen werden [. . .]?" (But we call many things 'existent' [*seiend*], and in different senses. Everything we talk about, mean, and are related to is in being in one way or another. What and how we ourselves are is also in being. Being is found in the fact and the manner of being, in *realitas*, in the presence-to-hand of things [*Vorhandenheit*], subsistence, validity, existence [*Da-sein*], and in the 'it gives' [*es gibt*][, too]. In *which* being is the meaning of being to be found; from which being is the disclosure of being to get its start?)[8] Here one hears, in fact, an echo of Brentano's question on the plurality (or here, the diversity) of the meanings of being, formulated by a recension composed as much of the traditional metaphysical meanings as of those, already in outline, that the existential analytic will bring out. But to this double list, *es gibt* has just been added, the literal sense of which we will retain— *it gives*—without covering over and concealing it with its usual English or French equivalents, *there is, il y a*, which are inexact though well established.[9] But the addition of this syntagma raises in itself a difficulty: for, if *es gibt* does not belong to the meanings of being, nor to the categories of beings, nor even to the lexicon of metaphysics, why has it just been added to their list? And furthermore, is it a term of the same rank as the others, or is it a new theme altogether? If the latter is the case, does it still belong to the question of beings and to the search for the meanings of being? The occurrences of *es gibt* that immediately follow offer no answer to these questions, because they stick to the preconceptual usage of everyday language.[10]

III

And yet, an interpolated clause provides a first indication: "Welt ist selbst nicht ein innerweltlich Seiendes, und doch bestimmt sie dieses Seiende so sehr, daß es nur begegnen und entdecktes Seiendes in seinem Sein sich zeigen kann, sofern es Welt 'gibt.' Aber wie 'gibt es' Welt?" (The world itself is not an innerworldly

THE REASON OF THE GIFT

being, and yet it determines innerworldly beings to such an extent that they can only be encountered and discovered and show themselves in their being because "it gives" the world. But how does "it give" the world?)[11] The being is discovered only in the world, precisely because it *is* only insofar as it is innerworldly, never without an already-opened world. From this transcendental anteriority of the world over the innerworldly being, it obviously follows that the world is not numbered among the innerworldly beings. And because only the being *is*, it is necessary to infer from this that the world, which is not a being, cannot properly be said to *be*. Thus we will not say that the world *is*, but rather, with all rigor, that "it gives" the world—that *es gibt* the world. A similar exclusion from being of that which cannot be defined as a being is specifically confirmed in §44, which summarizes the fundamental accomplishment of the first section of the published part, by enthroning *es gibt* as such in the existential analytic: "Sein—nicht Seiendes—'gibt es' nur, sofern Wahrheit ist. Und sie *ist* nur, sofern und solange Dasein ist. Sein und Wahrheit 'sind' gleichursprünglich." ("It gives" [*Es* gibt] being—not beings—only insofar as truth is. And truth *is* only because and as long as Da-sein is. Being and truth "are" equiprimordially.)[12] The first sentence confirms the preceding point: if only beings *are*, and if "so gewiß das Sein nicht aus Seiendem 'erklärt' werden kann [being certainly cannot be 'explained' in terms of beings],"[13] then being itself in the strict sense *is not*, but comes to pass by virtue of an *es gibt*. Conversely, *Dasein*, privileged as it may appear in relation to all other beings, still remains a being,[14] and thus one can say of it that it *is* (without quotation marks). This contrast, moreover, serves only to ratify a formula from §43: "Allerdings nur solange Dasein *ist*, das heißt die ontische Möglichkeit von Seinsverständnis, 'gibt es' Sein." (However, only as long as Da-sein *is*, that is, as long as there is the ontic possibility of an understanding of being, "it gives" [*gibt es*] being.)[15] At the risk of oversimplifying, it would be necessary to conclude that the difference (soon called ontological) between beings and being passes between that which *is* and that which *it gives*.

The second sentence of the passage from §44 extends to truth the privilege accorded to being: truth only *is* with a restriction, because it lines up equiprimordially with being, which itself *is* not, either; they only "are" with the restriction of quotation marks. Thus *es gibt* intervenes in the place and locus of *is* when the question is no longer that of a being, even a privileged one, but instead of being or of that which demands being's phenomenalization: first the world, then, as here, truth. Yet a certain ambiguity remains, especially seeing as this text still avails itself of typographical means in order to maintain that being "is," that truth *is*, and that the one and the other both "are." However, this ambiguity is corrected by an earlier statement from the same §44: "*Wahrheit 'gibt es' nur, sofern und solange Dasein ist.*" (*"It gives"* [*"gibt es"*] *truth only insofar as Da-sein is and as long as it is.)*[16] Thus, only the being (par excellence) with the rank of *Dasein* really is, whereas truth demands another procedure, an *es gibt*. To which one could doubtless add several quick indications concerning time. For the second section of the published part ends up putting into question just as clearly whether time can *be*, if not in its common and metaphysical sense: "Dabei blieb noch völlig unbestimmt, in welchem Sinne die ausgesprochene öffentliche Zeit '*ist*,' ob sie üperhaupt als *seiend* ansgesprochen werden kann." (We did not determine at all in what sense the public time expressed "is," or whether it can be addressed as *being* at all.)[17] As a matter of fact, it is necessary that time first find itself reduced (metaphysically) to presence, and then that presence itself be reduced to the present, and the present, in turn, to the instant, which is itself further supposed to be a point (Aristotle, Hegel), in order that time might come back to *be* in the strict sense, in this case in the sense of metaphysics. Inversely, a correct phenomenological analysis of time according to the original temporality of *Dasein* will speak solely of "die Zeit [. . .], die 'es gibt' [of time, that 'it gives']."[18]

Let us conclude provisionally: while one should obviously not read *Sein und Zeit* imprudently as anticipating *Zeit und Sein*, one can and even must recognize in them, among other com-

THE REASON OF THE GIFT

mon decisions, the following two: first, that being *is* no more than time *is*, because only a being can and must *be;* and second, that that which is not nevertheless gives itself—in other words, it phenomenalizes itself according to the *es gibt.* We find, then, a phenomenality of the *es gibt* (and, in this sense, of givenness, *Gegebenheit*), which approaches time and being in their inter-ference with one another, whereas the phenomenality of *is/ist* describes only *Dasein*'s involvement with other beings, whose being *Dasein* puts into play.

IV

Certainly, this conclusion may seem surprising. First, because the step back outside of metaphysics and its obstruction of the *Seinsfrage* would demand, paradoxically, the renunciation of the phenomenology of being, of the verb *is/ist/einai*, in order to at-tain a phenomenology that is, in fact, resolutely non-ontological (although not meontological), at least in the sense of the meta-physical *ontologia*. Next, the conclusion surprises because a pre-liminary question asserts itself: Does this step back from (or out in front of) *is/ist/einai*, and thus to the side of (or beyond) beings, arise from the possibilities of the phenomenological method as such—provided that this *as such* here retains any meaning? In outlining a shift toward the *es gibt*, does *Sein und Zeit* proceed simply by force, or does it in fact open out a possibility already implicitly inscribed within phenomenology? Asked another way, does its usage of *es gibt/it gives* remain without precedent and in-determinate, or does it achieve a previously glimpsed possibility of acceding to *Gegebenheit*?

It seems, in fact, that one might trace the usages of *es gibt* in *Sein und Zeit* back to three problematics nearly contemporary with *Gegebenheit*: (a) The thesis in §16 that beings "can only be encountered and discovered and show themselves in their being only for as much as 'it gives' the world [*sofern es Welt 'gibt'*]," such that one must first ask, "But how does 'it give' the world? [*wie 'gibt es' Welt?*],"[19] can be read as the taking up of one of Emil Lask's central theses: "Das *Gegebene* ist dabei nicht bloß das Sinnliche, sondern die ganze ursprüngliche Welt überhaupt, *woran* sich die kontemplative Formenwelt *aufbaut.* [. . .] Ursprünglich gibt es gar nicht 'Gegenstände,' sondern nur jenes Etwas, das kategorial gefaßt Gegenstand wird." (The *given*, therefore, is not the mere sensory, but the most original, complete world in general, *upon which* the intellectual world of forms *is erected.* [. . .] Originarily it does not give "objects," but only a something which, once grasped categorically, becomes an object.)[20] The original character of the *Gegebene* far surpasses the anteriority of the material and the sensory content *(das Sinnliche),* but results in nothing less than the world itself. And what we mean by the world consists precisely not in objects—for they do not compose the world, but instead become possible on its basis, which is always already given. (b) As for the passage from §2, which maintains that all the significations of the being *(l'étant)* find themselves dominated by the jurisdiction of *es gibt* ("Aber 'seiend' nennen wir vieles und in verschiedenem Sinne. [. . .] Sein liegt im Daß- und Sosein, in Realität, Vorhandenheit, Bestand, Geltung, Dasein, im 'es gibt.' An *welchem* Seienden soll der Sinn von Sein abgelesen werden [. . .]?"),[21] it takes on its full force if one reads it alongside what Rickert thematized under the title of the "universal form of givenness or factuality, die allgemeine Form der Gegeben*heit* oder Tatsächlich*keit.*"[22] He intended in this way to define within factuality itself a category, completely irreducible to the categories that define the matter or substance of the given, because it designates the very fact that the given finds itself given, and given in its individuality. For, Rickert insists, givenness, as mode of the given, rightfully demands its own category: "the category of givenness or factuality [*die Kategorie der Gegebenheit oder Tatsächlichkeit*]."[23] According to such a category, givenness indeed already determines every signification of beings, which also means that it precedes it. (c) There remain divisions 43–44, which, far from subsuming all ontico-ontological significations under the *es gibt,* have recourse to it only for being, truth, the world, and time, as opposed to all particular beings, including *Dasein.* Yet even this radical distinction finds a precedent in

Natorp. Indeed, if he admits givens, Natorp excludes the *I* itself from all givenness: "Datum hieße Problem; Problem aber ist das reine Ich eben nicht. Es ist Prinzip; ein Prinzip aber ist niemals 'gegeben,' sondern, je radikaler, um so ferner allem Gegebenen. 'Gegeben' würde überdies heißen 'Einem gegeben,' das aber hieße wiederum: Einem bewußt. Das Bewußt-sein ist im Begriff des Gegebenen also schon vorausgesetzt." (Given signifies problem; but the pure *I* is not a problem. It is a principle; now, a principle is never "given," but it is all the more radical in proportion to its remoteness from any given. Furthermore, "given" would mean "given to someone," which in turn would mean "conscious for someone." The conscious being thus finds itself presupposed in the concept of the given.)[24] Just as, in *Sein und Zeit, Dasein* above all does not arise from *es gibt*, for Natorp, the *I* is exempt from it. Of course, the difference between them is, for that, all the more visible: for Natorp, given signifies given as an object to consciousness, whereas for Heidegger, the object present-at-hand *(vorhanden)* conceals the innerworldly *es gibt* within itself. Nonetheless, it remains that Natorp's question is taken up by Heidegger, if only to find itself radically overturned, just as *Dasein* overturns the *I*.[25]

From this short overview, we can at least conclude that Heidegger in *Sein und Zeit* could by no means be unaware of the fact that his uses of *es gibt* took place within a strategic debate among his contemporaries about the status, situation, and breadth of *Gegebenheit*. All share one basic question: Should one define objects or beings? Should one start with an ontology or with a theory of the object? But this basic question is formulated by each of them against the background of a presupposition that remained implicit, even though it had seeped into all of the debates: Can one distinguish between objects and beings without first relating them to the givenness in them? No one saw or explained this better than Husserl, whose work was at the same time both conclusive for the neo-Kantian debate and inaugural of a new dispute with Heidegger.

V

In *Die Idee der Phänomenologie (The Idea of Phenomenology)*, the very text in which, in 1907, he for the first time and definitively asserts the operation of the reduction, Husserl puts the reduction to work for the sake of givenness. "Überall ist die Gegebenheit, mag sich in ihr bloß Vorgestelltes oder wahrhaft Seiendes, Reales oder Ideales, Mögliches oder Unmögliches bekunden, eine *Gegebenheit im Erkenntnisphänomen*, im Phänomen eines Denkens im weitesten Wortsinn." (Givenness is everywhere, whether it is announced by what is merely represented or by a true being, what is real or what is ideal, what is possible or what is impossible, [this givenness] is *a givenness within a phenomenon of cognition*, in the phenomenon of thought, in the widest sense of the term.)²⁶ Indeed, if "absolute givenness is the ultimate term [*absolute Gegebenheit ist ein Letztes*],"²⁷ it is the direct result of the reduction: "Erst durch eine Reduktion, die wir auch schon *phänomenologische Reduktion* nennen wollen, gewinne ich eine absolute Gegebenheit, die nichts von Transzendenz mehr bietet." (Only through a reduction, the same one we have already called *phenomenological reduction*, do I attain an absolute givenness which no longer owes anything to transcendence.)²⁸ We can't really distinguish Husserl from Natorp, Rickert, or Lask by his recourse to givenness, which they all have in common. He surpasses them by the condition he places on it—the operation of the reduction—which alone justifies the irreducibility of the given, truly irreducible because in fact resulting from the reduction. Given always signifies for Husserl given to cognition, to the *I* beneath the figure of a phenomenon, that is to say, according to the "wonderful" noetico-noematic "correlation [*wunderbaren Korrelation*]"²⁹ between the lived experiences of consciousness and the intentional object. This does not imply, as it does for Natorp, that the *I* simply remains the principle, outside of givenness, of a given comprehended as a simple fact, because the *I* itself has a role in the givenness in the consciousness of the temporal flux and its variations. Nor does this characterize givenness as an unjustified

THE REASON OF THE GIFT

category of factuality, as in Rickert, because phenomena that are neither factual nor effectual also give themselves—for example, logical idealities. Nor, finally, does this concern only the world, as for Lask, because even formal impossibilities, which are part of the world, may find themselves given.

Indeed, the very text that concluded with the fundamental declaration, "Überall ist die Gegebenheit [. . .] eine *Gegebenheit im Erkenntnisphänomen* [Everywhere givenness (. . .) is a *givenness within a phenomenon of cognition (knowledge)]*," develops a long list of the *"different modes of authentic givenness"*; it includes nearly all possible phenomena in givenness, among which are precisely those excluded by Natorp, Rickert, or Lask. Indeed, Husserl enumerates (a) "the givenness of the *cogitatio*," and (b) "the givenness of the *cogitatio preserved in a fresh recollection*"—thus, the *I* (against Natorp). Next, (c) "the givenness of the *unity of appearance* enduring in the phenomenal flux," (d) "the givenness of *change* itself," (e) "the givenness of *things* to the 'outer' sense," and (f) the givenness of various perceptions of the imagination and of memory. Overall, one could say that facts and beings of the world are at issue. But, Husserl adds, "naturally also [*natürlich auch*]," we must include in *Gegebenheit* (g) "*logical givenness*"—namely, "the givenness of *universals*, of *predicates*," and so on; and (h) therefore, in the end, even "the givenness of a *non-sense*, of a *contradiction*, of a *nothing*, etc. [auch die Gegebenheit eines *Widersinns*, eines *Widerspruchs*, eines *Nichtseins* usw.]."[30] Now, these last figures of givenness do not belong to the world (as Lask would have it), nor do they come under the category of factuality (following Rickert), nor do they constitute a fact of experience (as for Natorp). By what right, then, do non-sense, contradiction, and nothingness (or even the impossible) take a place within *Gegebenheit*? In effect, givenness becomes for Husserl universal exactly inasmuch as the reduction universally exercises its jurisdiction.

But from whence does it come that the things that do not figure as exceptions, specifically the impossible, non-sense, contradiction, and misunderstanding, still merit the title of given and also arise from givenness, since they exceed the limits of beings?

Must one conclude that *Gegebenheit* extends beyond *Seiendheit*, beyond the being as the possible of metaphysics?

VI

Husserl's decision becomes intelligible only by reference to a problem that was formulated but left open-ended by Bolzano in §67 of his *Wissenschaftslehre*, which is symptomatically titled "*Es gibt* auch gegenstandlose Vorstellungen [There Are (It Gives) also Objectless Ideas]." Bolzano, as we know, postulates that every representation has an object, a *something*, that it represents, "even the representation [thought] of nothing [*auch der Gedanke Nichts einen Stoff hat*]."[31] He proposes at least three examples: first, contradiction (a round square) and non-sense (green virtue), two unthinkable formal impossibilities; next, an impossibility of fact, strictly empirical, but not formally unthinkable (a mountain of gold). We note right away two determining points. (a) These three examples correspond to the ultimate extensions of givenness in Husserl. (b) In order to qualify these representations without objects, and which therefore surpass the limits of beingness, Bolzano has recourse to *es gibt* just as Husserl does to *Gegebenheit*. Properly speaking, one cannot say that "for Bolzano [. . .] 'nothing' doesn't 'exist' any less *insofar as it is a representation*,"[32] precisely because neither *being* nor *existing* extends to it, only givenness *(se donner/es gibt)*.

However, more so than through Bolzano and even Twardowski,[33] the connection between givenness and representations without objects was established by Meinong. Indeed, his 1904 *Theory of the Object (Gegenstandstheorie)* expressed it in the form of a celebrated paradox, which states that "it gives objects, about which it is valid to affirm that such objects do not give themselves [*es gibt Gegenstände, von denen gilt, daß es dergleichen Gegenstände nicht gibt*]."[34] Indeed, that which is not, either because it contradicts itself or because it has no signification, nonetheless remains a conceivable and conceived of object, even if only to find itself rejected as unreal, incomprehensible, or absurd: it remains an object exactly in that one must conceive it in order to recognize it precisely as not being. Thus even that which is not still comes under the object, since a theory, specifically, the theory of the object, has taken charge of it. Such an object is no longer defined by its being, nor even by its consistency *(Bestand, bestehen)* but by its givenness: "It does not give [*es gibt*] any object that, at least as a possibility, is not a potential object of knowledge. [. . .] Everything knowable is given [*ist gegeben*]—precisely to knowledge. Furthermore, insofar as all objects can be known, one can recognize without exception, whether they are or are not [*mögen sie sein oder nicht sein*], givenness [*die Gegebenheit*] as their most universal property."[35] Even the fact of withholding from at least possible knowledge by taking the status of object still implies no decision regarding the being of this object, or its possibility (its noncontradictory essence), or its position (its existence in the world), but requires only the minimum of givenness, of what *es gibt* assures. Above all one must not say that the object is in the mode of *es gibt,* because *Gegebenheit* dispenses it from being, to the point "that one might perhaps say that the pure object holds itself 'beyond being and non-being' [der reine Gegenstand stehe 'jenseits von Sein und Nichtsein']"; or that, insofar as given, it appears as "being outside of being [*außerseiend*]."[36] Thus, there emerges a science that is more comprehensive than metaphysics, since the latter limits itself to the region of that which is or can be (the possible), by excluding the impossible. As universal as it may be, the *ontologia* of *metaphysica generalis* still remains an "*a posteriori* science, which retains from the given for its research only that which can fall into line under the gaze of an empirical knowledge, which is to say, the whole of effectivity [eine aposteriorische, die vom Gegebenen so viel in Untersuchung zieht, als für empirisches Erkennen eben in Betracht kommen kann, die gesamte Wirklichkeit]." Another science, the theory of the object, precedes it and comprehends it, insofar as it confirms itself as truly "an *a priori* science, which takes into account all the given [*die alles Gegebene betrifft*]."[37]

Thus we must recognize in Meinong not only the merit of his having pushed the problem introduced by Bolzano to its paradoxical consequences, but above all his having neatly erected *Gegebenheit* as a more powerful and more comprehensive authority than *being*, at least as being is understood by the *ontologia* of metaphysics. Even that which is not—which is to say, what *cannot* be, because it does not accede to possibility—can be thought in the mode of the object, and thus, as such, something *given*. From Bolzano to Meinong, through what we roughly term neo-Kantianism, a gap thus opens between being and object. By saying *es gibt* where one cannot say *it is*, this gap allows for a step back *(Schritt zurück)*, outside of being, and perhaps outside of metaphysics as well.

VII

So the question no longer involves deciding whether or not givenness *(Gegebenheit, es gibt)* has the rank of a philosophical concept: the agreement of an entire tradition established it as one, such that Husserl, and also Heidegger, were able simply to inherit it.[38] But now a different, and doubtless more delicate, question arises: how should we interpret the gap that givenness opens up between itself and the being *(l'étant)* in the metaphysical sense? Kant clearly showed that beyond the metaphysical division (Suarez, Wolff) between the possible (the being, *ens*), and the impossible (nothingness, *nihil*), there had to be "a still higher [concept], and this is the concept of an object in general [*Gegenstand überhaupt*], taken problematically, without its having been decided whether it is something or nothing [*ob es etwas oder nichts ist*]."[39] But even Kant himself did not, in the end, decide on the ontological status (or lack thereof) of this "object in general." So what answers were offered to this question? Natorp, closest to Kant, tends to apply the given to all phenomena. Rickert and, in a sense, Lask, extend the given toward a transcendental determination (factuality, or the world). Twardowski and Meinong, and then Husserl, tend, in rather similar ways, to identify the object and the given, which are themselves set up as a universal determination of phenomenality.

But this very expansion does not go far before it gives rise to

THE REASON OF THE GIFT

a new difficulty. This is what it looks like in Husserl. When he claims to describe "the cardinal and principal difference between the domains of *consciousness* and *reality* [die prinzipielle Unterschiedenheit der Seinsweisen, die kardinalste, die es überhaupt gibt, die zwischen *Bewußtein* und *Realität*]," he thinks and defines it once again inside of the one and only givenness, speaking of "a *principal difference in the mode of givenness* [ein *prinzipieller Unterschied der Gegebenheitsart*]."[40] If even this differentiation leaves givenness undifferentiated, what specificity does it retain? And above all how is this universal undertaking reconciled with the caesura that the reduction implies? A certain ambiguity inevitably threatens the Husserlian *Gegebenheit:* if every object is based on the given, as at least all *possible* objects, in fact, *are*, then givenness would retain an intrinsic link with beings and would still remain a mode of being *(Seinsweise)* among others. The very universalization of *Gegebenheit*, at least as Husserl has achieved it, as a universalization of objectity *(Gegenständlichkeit)*, loses its radicality and weakens its breakthrough beyond being, *außerseiend.*[41]

By contrast, the strategic reversal of *Sein und Zeit* becomes evident. It is Heidegger's purpose to "destroy" the *ontologia* of metaphysics, which amounts to freeing himself from all ontology, above all from the ontology of the object (in other words, from the formal ontology of Husserl). This destruction is conducted by recourse to the existential analytic, where the mode of being of *Dasein* finds itself described, at first, at least, in strict opposition to the mode of being of objects and other innerworldly beings. In *this* sense, *Dasein is* not, at least in the sense that innerworldly beings are—and precisely are no longer, once anxiety opens *Dasein* to itself in the *Nichts.* How can we formulate clearly this step back outside the mode of being of innerworldly beings and of objects? By an extremely violent reversal, if one refers to givenness as a modality of *objects* (according to Bolzano, Twardowski, Natorp, Meinong, Husserl). For *Sein und Zeit*, in fact, *es gibt* not only no longer qualifies the object (whether impossible or general), but precisely all that which *is no longer,* in the sense of *ontologia* and of formal ontology, because its mode of being differs *ontologically* from all the other beings—*Dasein*, or rather all that which puts into operation its ontico-ontological privilege: truth, the world, time, and being. Heidegger thus turns the *es gibt* against the object, while his predecessors had invoked it in order to separate the object from (possible) beings. But they all, at least, had already agreed that givenness marks a border, which, in one way or another, puts the beingness of beings into question.

Thus givenness certainly has the status of a concept, because we can sketch its conceptual history. It does not pass only through Husserl and Heidegger, but also through all of neo-Kantianism, beginning with Bolzano's taking up of a question already sketched out by Kant. From *Wissenschaftslehre*, givenness passed, through *Erkenntnistheorie* and *Gegenstandstheorie*, to phenomenology and to the *Seinsfrage*. The question remains, today, to know if, in the final analysis, givenness might not arise from itself and from nothing else—not even from being or the *Ereignis*.

TWO

Remarks on the Origins of *Gegebenheit* in Heidegger's Thought

I

The course given by Heidegger from January to April of 1919,[1] during the *Kriegsnotsemester* (which one might translate as the "postwar emergency makeup semester"), in no way constitutes a debut for Heidegger, who, at this period, had already traversed a rather long and complex philosophical itinerary. But it neverthe-less constitutes a new beginning: certainly because it offers to a young veteran the opportunity to introduce other veterans to philosophy. A risky opportunity, considering that what it was to be about—the gap between academic theoretical philosophy and life itself—had just been endured by everyone, in their souls, and thus in their flesh, and all the more since this was under the figure of death. Above all, a new beginning because Heidegger made this existential gap his theme and expounded upon it in a reso-lutely dramatic manner: "Already in the opening of the question 'Gibt es—Does it give?,' it gives something. Our *entire* problem-atic has arrived at a crucial point, which, however, appears insig-nificant and even miserly. [. . .] We are standing at the method-ological cross-road which will decide on the very life or death of philosophy. We stand at an abyss: either into nothingness, that is, absolute reification, pure thingness [*absoluten Sachlichkeit*], or we somehow leap into *another world*, more precisely, we manage for the first time to make the leap into the world as such" (*GA* 56/57, §13, 63; *TDP,* 51, trans. modified). Thus, the philosophical question, in this dramatic postwar context, is decidedly posed under the heading of the *es gibt*, which is to say givenness, *Gegebenheit*.

In other words: by saying "Es gibt—it gives," one reaches a point that is certainly determinant, but determinant precisely insofar as it remains through and through indeterminant; for the issue is not that of a conquest, but of a test, where one must choose between two orientations, all the more incompatible with one another in that each one claims to decide everything. On one side, philosophy as the knowledge of things, and on the other, philosophy as the entryway into the experience of the world— and between the two, no compromise. Moreover, confirming this dilemma, the winter 1919–20 course will formulate the same choice in terms that are almost just as pressing: "The problem of givenness [*der Gegebenheit*] is not a particular [and] specific problem. With it, the paths of the modern doctrines of knowledge diverge from one another and, at the same time, [they diverge] from phenomenology, which must first deliver the problem from a restricted problematic of epistemology [*aus einer verengenden erkenntnistheoretischen Problematik*]."[2] The destiny of philosophy thus would turn upon givenness and upon the simple "It gives"; philosophy would become either one of the doctrines of knowledge, or phenomenology.

How then could the ever-so-simple question, "Gibt es . . . ?" become so radical and all encompassing? In order to attempt to glimpse an answer, let us note first of all that the lines that we have just read open section 13 of the course from 1919; they therefore must be placed alongside the last lines of section 12, which immediately precede them. Now, this section 12 in fact concludes with a double question: "Does it give [*gibt es*] even a single thing, if it only gives things? Then it gives absolutely no thing at all; it gives not even *nothing*, because with the sole supremacy of the sphere of things it no longer even gives 'it gives.' Does it give the 'it gives'—*Gibt es das 'es gibt'*?" (*GA* 56/57, §12, 62; *TDP* 48, trans. modified). This prior questioning thus confirms the subsequent thesis that neither the *Es gibt* nor *Gegebenheit* constitutes, as such, a solution or an advance, but offers indeed only a question. Moreover, Heidegger will name it, in 1919–20, as such, as the *"problem of givenness."*[3] Even more than a question, the issue is ultimately the indication that, henceforward, one can no longer dodge a question, which nevertheless has yet to be formulated: "What does it mean to say 'given,' *'givenness'*—this magic word of phenomenology, and the 'stumbling block' for the others?"[4] How does *Gegebenheit* come to separate first of all the theories of knowledge [*Erkenntnistheorie*] among themselves (in the above quotation, "the others"), and then these from phenomenology— the former entangling themselves in *Gegebenheit* and the latter invoking it without truly understanding it? How does the question about *Es gibt* indicate the crossroads where the paths cross that lead either toward thingness or toward the world? The seriousness of this question is confirmed in the continuation that Heidegger assigns it in 1919, when he asks whether, in the end, the question itself, "Does it give [*gibt es*]?" might not contradict itself to the point of preventing that it give, if it merely gives.[5]

An initial conclusion is evident at the outset: it is not enough simply to appeal to the syntagm "it gives—*es gibt*" to wrest philosophy from the primacy and the fascination, in short, from the "omnipotence of thingness." "The domain of originarity [*das Ursprungsgebiet*] must not be given; it remains first to be conquered."[6] For, if by *es gibt* one believes that he will reach givenness, *Gegebenheit*, directly, without taking care to define it, or even to interrogate it more deeply, then, since givenness itself already holds a common and well-known philosophical meaning, even the pure springing forth of "it gives" could easily lead back, ultimately, only to thingness. And Heidegger does not hesitate to draw this conclusion, when he stigmatizes the " 'given— *gegeben*,' " saying that it "already signifies an inconspicuous but genuine theoretical reflection inflicted upon the environment. Thus 'givenness—*Gegebenheit*' is very well already a theoretical form," because, put another way, " 'givenness—*Gegebenheit*' signifies the initial objectifying infringement of the environment [*Umweltlichen*]" (*GA* 56/57, §17, 89; *TDP* 69). In short, "it gives—*es gibt*" might very well not open, but instead prevent access to itself and to givenness. We will understand better why if we see that here, quite evidently, Heidegger is alluding to Natorp and to Rickert, respectively.

II

How does the 1919 course consider Natorp, to whom all of its section 19 is devoted? Clearly, givenness plays a role, but within the theoretical attitude, so as to ensure to the constitution of objects (and its activity) a (passive) given at the outset, which only remains a given by confirming itself in the position that thought then assigns it, as is evident in the following, singled-out quotation: "To a givenness there must correspond an active *giving*,"[7] that is to say, the spontaneity of the understanding reconstructing the object beginning from the pre-theoretical immediacy, but provisionally so. The 1919–20 course soon specifies this verdict: for Natorp, "Nowhere is it a question of speaking of a finished and given object. *Before* every givenness stands thought and its conformity to law [*Gesetzlichkeit*]."[8] Such that the "givenness springs forth only from the determination. The establishing thought has an absolute privilege. [. . . T]o set up in thought. It gives *nothing pre-given*." Givenness is only established by letting itself be taken up by the thought that objectivizes it and thus cancels it: "The given itself is a given-up [*Das Gegebene selbst ist ein Aufgegebenes*]."[9] Indeed, if one turns directly to other texts of Natorp, the subordination of givenness to thought, and thus to the spontaneity of the legislating understanding, is confirmed without any ambiguity: "Nor can the *I* of pure consciousness be properly called a '*datum*' of psychology. *Datum* means problem; but the pure *I* is absolutely not a problem. It is a principle; a principle is never 'given,' but, the more radical it is, the more distant from every given. 'Given' would moreover mean 'given to someone [*Einem gegeben*],' and, as we see again, to someone conscious. The conscious being is what, in its very concept, the given already presupposes. But it is precisely as the presupposition of any givenness that pure consciousness cannot itself be said to be 'given'; no more than the appearing could itself be said to be an appearance [*das Erscheinen . . . eine Erscheinung*]."[10] The *I*, or rather what is always already the "pure consciousness," precedes the given and allows its appearing—thus it exempts itself from the appearing as from the given. It is indeed necessary to go that far: the *I* effectively has no relation whatsoever with phenomenality, nor with givenness, because it grounds them. The grounding does not appear in what it grounds, just as it does not give itself, because the given presupposes it. Natorp does not hesitate to draw, with the utmost clarity, this "paradoxical consequence, that the original *I*, the pure *I*, the *I* of consciousness [*Bewußtheit*] [. . .] is neither a fact, nor an existent, nor a phenomenon. But the paradox disappears as soon as one realizes that it is the ground of all facts, the ground of all existence, of all being-given [*alles Gegebenseins*], of all appearing; it is only for that that it cannot itself be either a fact, nor an existence, nor a given, nor something that appears [*ein Erscheinendes sein*]."[11] Thus, givenness is only mobilized to submit itself to pure consciousness, which, through the activity of "reconstruction," raises it to the rank of an object. It only appears in order to disappear in its double contrary. Thus, according to Heidegger, or rather according to Natorp, for the school of Marburg, givenness only emerges in order to be, in fact, immediately dissolved, because thought and its primacy do not, within the objectity of the theoretical attitude, leave it any rightful legitimacy.

The 1919 course opposes to Natorp above all the already legendary figure of Lask. Nevertheless, we will not dwell on this development here, first of all precisely because Lask's very importance renders his figure ambiguous, so much does Heidegger see in Lask what the war prevented Lask from becoming: "one of the strongest philosophical personalities of our time, [. . .] who in my view was on the way to phenomenology" (*GA* 56/57, §9, 180; *TDP* 137); and also, because an examination of Lask's position and his relation to Heidegger, which remains to be completed, would require work of a very different scope.[12] We shall instead line up Rickert, rather than Lask, against Natorp, first of all because Lask himself (as much as Heidegger) derives from Rickert and in part leads back to him;[13] and, next, because the 1919–20 course refers to him in order to establish a contrast to Natorp. Indeed, Rickert is different from Natorp, according to Heidegger's assessment, because he recognizes that "the factual, the 'perceived' ['*Wahrgenommene*'] is given—it is what is experienced immediately [. . .] something ultimate, underivable, 'irrational' ";[14] for example, blue or red, which can never more, once given, "vanish in a rationalist mode."[15] For, after all, and definitively, it must be agreed that: "It gives [*es gibt*] particular givennesses [*bestimmte Gegebenheiten*], that one cannot fail to recognize."[16] And for Rickert, in fact, it is necessary to say, beyond the object in general (which *Erkenntnistheorie*, like *ontologia*, privileges), it gives *such* an object in its actual facticity, for "that there be a color means nothing other than: the color is a fact, is given, is perceived."[17] Thus, this implies not only an aiming at the *this* as such, but accepting the *this* itself as a form which is universally applicable to every fact, and thus accepting "the form of the *individual* real given or the form of affirmation of judgment, which establishes a real given that is factual, individual, and determined *each time*."[18] At issue, then, is not a category of the given in general (another name for the object in general), but a universal category of the given as individual and unique: "it certainly does not give any [*es gibt zwar keine*] individual forms and norms, but it gives *forms and norms of the individual*,"[19] not a category of actuality in general, but "a category of real *this-being-here* [*des realen Dieseins*]."[20]

And yet, what exactly is involved in Rickert's attempt to "understand givenness as a category"[21] or, more precisely, as a "*category of givenness or of factuality*"?[22] Heidegger marks out two different conclusions. First, this debate allows one to distinguish in reality two primary meanings of givenness: on one side that of Natorp, who only allows "a givenness [*Gegebenheit*] that derives in a precise sense from the accomplishment of science [*der Leistung der Wissenschaft*]," and thus remains within it without exempting itself from it; on the other that of Rickert, who allows "a givenness [*Gegebenheit*] that is *anteriorly-given* [*vorgegeben*], by necessity of meaning, to this accomplishment [of science] and its possible use [*ihrem möglichen Einsatz*]."[23] Thus we understand better in what way givenness was marking out a crossroads in philosophy, a crossing of paths, where two accepted meanings of *Erkenntnistheorie* diverge, according to whether the given is inscribed within the knowledge of the object or precedes and determines it irreducibly. There remains another conclusion: Heidegger said that the crossing of paths distinguishes not only two postulations of *Erkenntnistheorie* from one another but also these two from phenomenology.[24] Can we now articulate this second opposition? Certainly, if we pay attention to a "*confusion* [*eine Verwechslung*]" made by Rickert: the given having remained for him a given of judgment, and thus for the knowing subject, he thinks of it only in terms of the immanent, of the "content of consciousness" (the *datum* of color), and "confuses" it with "the color on the wall (transcendent)"—or rather prefers it and substitutes it for the color on the wall. Thus, givenness regresses from the transcendence of "factical experience" to the peaceful, banal, and representative immanence of a lived experience of consciousness (to the "givenness of an immanent [*eines Immanenten*], or a content of consciousness"). Here is precisely where Rickert turns away from the path of phenomenology. Neither he nor Natorp "procedes from factical experience [*faktischen Erfahren*]." They thus miss "the *new fundamental experience of life in and for itself*."[25] How can we explain this disqualification of givenness, no sooner accepted?

Doubtless it is precisely because *Gegebenheit* was thematized as a "category." Now, a category can only allow a judgment and a predication; it thus can only bear upon things ("the category of givenness or of factuality, *Tatsächlichkeit*"). Henceforward, even if it finds itself being thought as *Tatsächlichkeit*, how could givenness not fall back immediately under "the supremacy of the sphere of things [*der Sachsphäre*]" (*GA* 56/57, §12, 62; *TDP* 48)? It never left it.

III

Thus the true difficulty emerges: if givenness still decides nothing, since it can also lead, or indeed most often leads, to the "nothingness" of thingness rather than to a leap in the world's direction, it must be granted that the "it gives—*es gibt*" itself remains undecided. If from the outset it is allowed to be taken back by the horizon of things alone (put otherwise, if it only gives things), then, to the extent that a thing can be phenomenalized fully only in a world, *will it give* even one single thing if it only gives things without the world, *according to thingness alone*? What is more: if no thing is found to be truly given, then it will in fact give "nothing" (*GA* 56/57, §12, 62; *TDP* 48), and thus it will give "nothingness" (§13, 63; *TDP* 51). And if it gives nothing, it will not give at all—not even the "it gives." In the end, it is unavoidable to ask whether, in the already theoretical and thingly meaning of "it gives," the "it gives" itself does not disappear. Indeed, one might elaborate a bit by saying that if "it only gives *this* 'it gives,' then it doesn't even give a true 'it gives.'" In other words, the choice, the border, and the crossing of paths pass not between givenness and *es gibt*, on the one hand, and the thing, on the other, but, instead, within the "it gives" itself, according to whether it opens upon the thing or upon a world. At the outset, Heidegger thus frees himself from the myth of the given,[26] from the fetishism of givenness as a category, and even from the nevertheless radical appearance of the operation of "it gives." From the beginning, he stigmatizes their undecided status and requires that a decision be made about them from a point of view transcendent to them. Which point of view? We will answer, provisionally and approximatively: from a point of view that is as strictly phenomenological as possible.

The point, then, is to conceive what "it gives" might mean: "Was heißt: 'es gibt'?" (*GA* 56/57, §13, 67; *TDP* 54). Not existing, valuing, duty, accomplishing, contradicting (all cardinal terms of neo-Kantianism), but "giving" in an "it gives." Not the being in general, nor such and such a being (a Rembrandt, a Mozart sonata, a chair or a table, houses or trees, a submarine or a religious power), but that which gives itself in "it gives." Indeed, "it gives" gives nothing in particular, and the point is not "to return to understand [or grasp] particular objects" (68; *TDP* 54, trans. modified), even if this regressive movement, which causes the "it gives" to be missed, may seem almost inevitable. We must, on the contrary, grant that "it gives" as such is equivalent to asking, "does it give *something* [*etwas*]?" (67; *TDP* 54, trans. modified). And this question in turn involves envisaging an "*anything whatsoever* [*etwas überhaupt*]" (68; *TDP* 54). In absolute terms, with what generality are we here concerned? How do we not unavoidably think of formal ontology's "something in general = X," or of its equivalents, "the formal objective *something of knowability* [, . . . the] something of formal theoretization" (§20, 116; *TDP* 88)? How do we avoid inscribing it right away, ever and again, within the most abstract relation between object and subject, precisely as the minimum abstract object for a particular subject? So much does it seem obvious that "'it gives' means: it gives *for me the questioner*" (§13, 68; *TDP* 55, trans. modified).

All of Heidegger's paradoxical and almost impracticable effort consists in establishing that, precisely here, such is no longer the case: in the "it gives," contrary to the evidence of the theory of knowledge, it is no longer (or not yet) a question of a relation of subject to object. First of all, because we no longer find here even the slightest "subject" to master a knowledge: "nothing like an 'I' is found [*nicht so etwas wie ein 'Ich'*]" (66; *TDP* 53, trans. modified), "I do not find anything like an 'I'" (68; *TDP* 55). Let us take the example of the lectern, from which the professor addresses his students—and here Heidegger describes the very situation in which he and his students find themselves at the moment in which he is speaking, such that they become for themselves the phenomenological example to consider; let us ask whether, in this case, the fact that it gives the lectern implies that it gives it either to any old *I*, or to such and such other *I*, to such and such master's or doctoral student, to a certain doctor of philosophy, or to a postdoc in law. Clearly (or at least according to the clarity that Heidegger sees and wants to make visible), the fact that it gives the lectern opens no relation whatsoever to an *I*, no more to mine than to that of any other person: "the meaning of the lived experience has no relation with any particular *I*" (69; *TDP* 55, trans. modified). Certainly, it does give itself to me—the lectern as that which becomes visible to me also indeed appears to me—but without any relation to any particular *I* being required and implied in this "ex-perience of something [*Er-leben von etwas*]" (68; *TDP* 55). In short, "I experience it vitally [*er-lebe*], it belongs to *my* living [*Leben*], but it is still so detached from me in its sense, so absolutely far from the 'I,' so '*I*-remote' [*absolut Ich-fern*]" (69; *TDP* 55, trans. modified), that it convokes no *I*, nor does it submit itself to one. In other words, the phenomenon that nevertheless directly implies in itself the orator and his auditors, that is to say the lectern, nevertheless does not refer to the least *I* as the necessary condition for its appearance or its meaning; as a consequence, neither does it open any access to one in return. The phenomenon, such that "it gives [it]," does not depend upon an *I*, any more than it leads back to one. "The 'it gives' is indeed an 'it gives' for an I—and yet it is not *I* to and for *whom* the question relates" (69; *TDP* 55, trans. modified). The lectern gives itself, and so it is assigned to no one. Thus a first characteristic of "it gives" emerges (which definitively distinguishes it from the theoretical attitude): the *I*, which remains affected by the lectern, nevertheless remains the simple addressee of givenness, but not its author; it finds itself there as that to whom the lectern befalls, though not as the one who determines its movement or its stakes. In short, I depend upon the "es gibt," but it depends no more on me than does that which it gives me to experience. Thus, as under the blow of a reduction, a first term of the theoretical relation, the subject, falls and finds itself bracketed.

But, more essentially, there is no longer any subject to be found because there is already no longer any object to be found here. What, precisely, appears when the lectern that none of them, neither students nor professor, constitutes rises up before their eyes? What do they really see? Do they see planks, a frame, or even a stand and a box laid upon the desk? In fact, they no more see these elements (which nevertheless are there) than they see colors, shadows, and supposed secondary qualities (§16, 81; *TDP* 64), nor, inversely, than they see pieces of such and such wood (of such "essences"), ligneous molecules or atoms of carbon, and so on (which are also there). They see "in one fell swoop" (§14, 71; *TDP* 57) the lectern itself. And in fact, they see it precisely because they perceive from the outset what its function is (it is for the course), who presides there (the professor), what goes with it (the book and notes), what it delivers (concepts, information, etc.); in short, they see it because they perceive there from the outset the action of the professor teaching students. What thus appears has nothing of an object about it, nor even of a thing; from the outset, and first of all, what is at issue is an "object as fraught with meaning [*als mit einer Bedeutung behaftet*]" (71; *TDP* 57), with "a meaning [. . .], a moment of signification [*ein bedeutungshaftes Moment*]" (72; *TDP* 58); because "the meaningful [*das Bedeutsame*] is primary and immediately given to me without any mental detours across thing-oriented apprehension" (73; *TDP* 58). The meaning is given, because it shows itself without an object and before every objectification.[27]

Let us suppose a counterexample: that it gives the lectern to someone (Heidegger supposes a Senegalese—why this strange choice?) who has never seen one, and thus does not know by any experience what it is for, nor what it has to do with—who thus does *not* recognize this precise signification of a university lectern; indeed, one cannot say that he sees the lectern by first seeing its signification, because in effect he has absolutely no notion at all of this signification. But must we therefore conclude that he sees nothing at all, or again an object, reducible either to secondary qualities or to its material components? Clearly, no. Either he will see another signification, proper to his culture and his customary environmental milieu (for example, an element of domestic worship, a sign of social recognition, a marker of religious power, etc.)—in short, another signification acceptable for him, who is "not culture-less" (§15, 72; *TDP* 58), even if that signification doesn't match mine. Or, he will see nothing more than the "instrumental strangeness [*zeuglichen Fremdseins*]" itself; but this still remains, at its core, identical to that which I see as the lectern, the lectern seen as signification, because the issue is still that of a "meaningful character [*Bedeutungshafte*]" (§14, 72; *TDP* 58, trans. modified)—even a negative one.

Thus "that which it gives" is given with recourse neither to a subject nor to an object. The lectern, for instance, is not given by me, for I do not constitute it on the basis of some such (psychological) given immediate to my consciousness; it springs up and imposes itself, so to speak, beginning from itself as its pure signification. Neither does it give itself as an object, which I might reconstitute beginning from its most basic (physical) components, such as they are analyzed by the theoretical attitude (atoms, particles, molecules, etc.) (§17, 84–86; *TDP* 66–68). How, then, does "that which it gives" succeed in freeing itself from the two extremes between which is enacted not only the final state of metaphysics, as illustrated endlessly by Heidegger's contemporaries before his very eyes, but also the whole theoretical attitude and its ever-so-powerful empire? First and above all insomuch as that which it gives, gives in no way an object to see, nor even a thing, but directly the surrounding world itself: "In the experience of seeing the lectern something is given *to me* from out of an immediate environment [*gibt sich* mir *etwas aus einer unmittelbaren Umwelt*]" (§14, 72; *TDP* 58); and it is by "living in an environment [*einer Umwelt*] [that] it signifies [*bedeutet*] to me everywhere and always" (§14, 73; *TDP* 58); for "the meaningful signification [*das Bedeutungshafte*]" is equivalent in the end to "the meaningful dimension of the environing world [*Umweltcharakter*]" (§17, 86; *TDP* 68). This term, neither subjective nor objective, precisely designates what all of metaphysics in its terminal phase (under the banners of realism or of idealism) does not want to, and cannot, grant.

And so, we can now understand the initial questioning of the reach of "es gibt." For the "it gives [*es gibt*]" and, what is more, "givenness [*Gegebenheit*]," keep within themselves and in themselves as such, their dangerous ambiguity, because they are in no way enough to guarantee access to the *Umwelt* as such. Indeed, in their current, that is to say metaphysical, accepted meaning, the operation that these terms put into motion can easily function for the primacy of theory and thus of objectivity: "*How do I live and experience [erlebe ich] the environment? How* is it 'given' to me? No, for something environmental to be *given* is already a theoretical infringement. It is already forcibly removed from me, from my historical 'I'; the 'it worlds [es weltet]' is already no longer primary. 'Given' already signifies an inconspicuous but genuine theoretical reflection inflicted upon the environment. Thus 'givenness' is already altogether a theoretical form" (§17, 88–89; *TDP* 69, trans. modified). Thus one speaks of immediate givens and of perceived qualities, "but all in the mode of the thing [*dinghaft*]. Space is thing-space, time is thing-time" (89; *TDP* 70, trans. modified). And the assumed immediacy of givens already destroys the *Umwelt*, to the benefit of the assumed elementary components of the object to come (85; *TDP* 67). In this context of an almost irrepressible and nearly imperceptible drift, "'givenness' signifies the initial objectifying infringement of the environment [*vergegenständlichende Antastung des Umweltlichen*], its initial placement before the *still* historic 'I'" (89; *TDP* 69). For, in response to the thingification of the *Umwelt* and of the phenomenon that worlds itself in an immediate given, the *I* slowly but surely loses its historicity. In other words, "the historical 'I' is de-historicized [*das historische Ich ist ent-geschichtlicht*] into the residue of a specific 'I-ness' as the correlate of thingliness" (89; *TDP* 70). With the "it gives," at least if one conceives it on the basis of givenness reduced to the rank of a category, the *Umwelt* loses its own (nontheoretical) phenomenality, which bursts into two parallel and originally indissociable secondary fragments: that of the *I* into a (constituent) correlate of the object, and that of the signification appearing at once in the reality of the thing, and then soon after as a (constituted) object.

Now the *Umwelt*, on the contrary, can and must only be experienced (*erleben*); and that is only possible "in the essence of life in and for itself"; otherwise, the theoretical attitude can take it back under its sway—and so easily (88; *TDP* 69)! It is necessary to strive conversely to understand the "it gives" itself beginning from and under the aegis of "it worlds." For it also remains "the basic statement of essence: all that is real can 'world,' but not all that 'worlds' need be real." Such that what "worlds," that which appears in the mode of "it worlds," to wit, the worldhood of the environment *(das Umweltliche)*, "has its own mode of self-demonstration in itself" (91; *TDP* 71, trans. modified). Which one? Only one answer, still provisional, and still negative, comes prior to *Sein und Zeit:* it demonstrates itself by allowing itself to be experienced: "The 'something' as the pre-worldly as such must not be conceived theoretically [. . .]. It is a basic phenomenon that can be experienced in the mode of understanding [*ein Grundphänomen, das verstehend erlebt werden kann*]" (§20, 115; *TDP* 88, trans. modified). Or again, the " 'it worlds' is not established theoretically, but is experienced as 'worlding' " (§17, 94; *TDP* 73). This can be formulated yet again negatively by saying: "All theoretical comportment [. . .] is de-vivifying [*Alles theoretische Verhalten [. . .] ist ein entlebendes*]" (§18, 100; *TDP* 78); and here *ein ent-lebendes* will be understood at the same time according to the meaning of that which rids itself of life and that which undoes the experience of the lived. But it can also be positively formulated by saying, "Leben ist historisch" (§20, 117; *TDP* 90), on the condition that we also understand in this *Leben* not only *living* but, in an essential counterpoint, *Erleben*, the *experiencing* that it *(Leben)* alone makes possible.

To mark the radical approach to "it gives" and tear it from its not only often possible but primarily and mostly inevitable theoretical drift, Heidegger resorts to a radical criterion. In fact, what we are talking about here is something like a marker, which anticipates with a rather stunning audacity the final steps of Heidegger's path of thought. When I experience *(Erlebnis)*, for instance, the professor's lectern, which is phenomenalized at once as a signification and not as a thing or a constituted object, the "experience [. . .] is not a process but rather an *event of appro-*

priation [*Ereignis*] (non-process, or in the experience of the question a residue of this event, *Ereignis*). Lived experience [*das Erleben*] does not pass in front of me like a thing that I establish, like an object, but rather I appropriate it to myself [*er-eigne es mir*], and it appropriates [*er-eignet*] itself according to its essence" (§15, 75; *TDP* 60, trans. modified). In other words, "If the experiences of other subjects have reality at all, then this can only be as proper events of appropriation [*Er-eignisse*], and they can only be evident as such events, i.e. as appropriated [*als Er-eignisse, als ge-eignet*] by an historical 'I'" (§16, 78; *TDP* 62). Indeed, more than a still-undetermined anticipation, the issue here is the same decision that seems to traverse and sustain Heidegger's entire trajectory. For, in the quasi-conclusive text of 1962, *Zeit und Sein*, when Heidegger takes up for the last time the meditation upon "it gives, *es gibt*," deploying there, it is true, a phenomenological mastery far outstripping the approximations of 1919, the task is still to think "it gives" not only independently of thingliness and theoretical objectity but especially, this time, beyond being and time. And, here again, the same marker, the *Ereignis*, comes in to guarantee the correct understanding of "it gives." At issue is the strongest, and therefore the most debatable, thesis: "Being vanishes in the *Ereignis*."[28] The *Ereignis* would thus constitute the phenomenological correction that, from one extreme to the other, ensures, in Heidegger's eyes, the phenomenological (and not the theoretical) approach to "it gives, *es gibt*."

Thus it is this correction that should be discussed when measuring just how far Heidegger led the phenomenology of givenness, and at what point he foreclosed it.

THREE

Substitution and Solicitude

HOW LEVINAS RE-READS HEIDEGGER

*We do not die each for ourselves, but for one another, or even, who knows,
one in place of another.*—Georges Bernanos, *Dialogues des Carmélites*, III, 1

I. THE QUESTION OF HYPERBOLE

The powerful originality of the thought of Emmanuel Levinas makes itself felt on each page of his oeuvre, all the more as time passes. But perhaps it never asserts itself more powerfully than with the relatively late doctrine (introduced between 1968 and 1974) of substitution. Paul Ricoeur, condemning what he called a "strategy" of "accumulation of *excessive, hyperbolic* expressions, destined to baffle common thinking," saw substitution as "crowning this sequence of excessive expressions."[1]

A surprising doctrine indeed, because it involves a redoubling of responsibility—put another way, "one *more* responsibility"[2]—such that I substitute myself for the other precisely in what he has that is most properly his own, his own responsibility: "the overemphasis of openness is responsibility for the other to the point of substitution."[3] What is more, at issue is not a mere hyperbole of responsibility, where I would take upon myself the burden that properly belongs to the other out of sympathy, scruple, or solidarity. Instead, at issue is first of all "a responsibility with regard to men we do not even know,"[4] or even, "responsibility for the persecutor" himself.[5] A strange and shocking assertion! Strange, for, if there were a man we knew well and whose face we should never forget (supposing that he has one),[6] wouldn't he be, precisely, our persecutor? Shocking, too, for how could we take upon ourselves the responsibility for a fault committed against us? We already experience great difficulty in not clamoring for revenge; how would we bear the difficulty of taking upon ourselves—of taking upon myself, the victim—the fault of the persecutor? And why must we? For in the end, wouldn't such a demand—"In the trauma of persecution [. . .] to pass from the outrage undergone to the responsibility for the persecutor"[7]—betray a perversion of ethics, now become a mechanism for condemning the victims in the place and stead of the executioners? In the end, how could this demand not contradict the famous dedication of *Otherwise than Being:* "To the memory of [. . .] the victims of the same hatred of the other man, the same anti-semitism"?[8]

I will attempt to show that, in the final instance, there is no contradiction whatsoever to be found here, nor an excess of hyperbole, but instead a purely conceptual necessity, paradoxical as it may be. Indeed, in order to avoid degrading substitution to a mere rhetorical effect (whether one approves or deplores it), it is necessary to see that its brutality results from the encounter of two lexicons and of two modes of questioning, which play like two telluric plates at once opposing and supporting each other— that is, one lexicon that belongs to phenomenology and one that depends upon what one could call, for lack of a better name, the revelation of the infinite. And indeed, how could one say, as Levinas did in the conclusion of his 1974 book, that *Otherwise than Being* "ventures beyond phenomenology" (trans. Lingis, 183), if not because substitution fixes precisely the second focus of the ellipse, with the first focus remaining the phenomenological *I* (transcendental, or perhaps also *daseinsmässig*)? Two declarations offer unambiguous confirmation. "The overemphasis of openness is responsibility for the other to the point of substitution, where the *for-the-other* proper to disclosure, to monstration to the other, turns into the *for-the-other* proper to responsibility. This is the thesis of the present work." And: "This book interprets the *subject* as a *hostage* and the subjectivity of the subject as a substitution breaking with being's *essence*."[9] In short, what is first of all and radically at stake in substitution is subjectivity.

Thus it could not be said more clearly: substitution (which

constitutes me as a "hostage," a term still to be defined) does not first fall under an ethical horizon, because it has as its more radical task the contradiction of the primacy of the *I*, that is to say, the determination of subjectivity by an essence, and thus by being. At issue here is not yet, once again, ethics (which determines how subjectivity should act in order to render justice to the other), but a prior task, otherwise difficult—that of freeing subjectivity from any ontological determination (of identifying, for instance, which subjectivity acts when the question is the rendering of justice). Here we find exactly verified a paradox advanced several years later: "My task does not consist in constructing ethics; I only try to find its meaning. [. . .] One can without doubt construct an ethics in function of what I have just said, but this is not my own theme."[10] For, even and above all if one establishes ethics as first philosophy, one must recognize that this establishment itself could not fall under ethics, since ethics profits thereby. Or else, one must understand "a concept of the ethical [*Begriff des Ethischen*] that is separated from the tradition that derives the ethical [*das Ethische*] from knowledge and from Reason."[11] In which case, just as substitution exceeds ethics itself, the term subjectivity must no longer be understood here according to ontology, even when inverting it, and even less according to what metaphysics understands under the title of ethics.[12]

Subjectivity must itself become a question, so as to allow itself precisely to be rethought beginning from substitution, and so perhaps to conceive the ethical element non-metaphysically: "Subjectivity is being hostage. This notion reverses the position where the presence of the ego to itself appears as the beginning or as the conclusion of philosophy."[13] As soon as one ceases to hear it in its ethical sense, substitution loses its strange hyperbolic quality, because it assumes from that point forward an eminent and nonethical function—that of putting into question the "essence of being," as "philosophy" (metaphysics and even phenomenology) presupposes it for defining man's "subjectivity." Substitution must thus be understood here in the *extra-moral sense* of a radical reversal of ontology by the bias of a destruction of all determination according to the being of what is at issue in subjectivity. Thus understood, "ethics" (the ethical element) opens a way toward an ipseity without being.

II. A DEBATE WITH *SEIN UND ZEIT*, §26

But where does Levinas's notion of substitution come from? The point here is not to reconstitute its lexical provenance, which in itself is of little importance (supposing, of course, that it could be traced); rather, my goal is to zero in on the operation, the impact, and the stakes that could qualify substitution, to the point where it would assume such a polemical role in so vast a "destruction."

The hypothesis I wish to suggest is the following: the question of substitution is posed to Levinas by Heidegger himself, in section 26 of *Sein und Zeit*. Indeed, Heidegger would not have held and retained until the end, and despite all his faults, such prestige in Levinas's eyes[14] if the existential analytic had merely missed the question of the other. However, contrary to a widely shared opinion, *Sein und Zeit* does not pass over in silence the question of the other, even if the other does not occupy in the book the center of the question of being. The border between Heidegger and Levinas does not pass between, on the one hand, a *Dasein* without alterity and, on the other, an *ego (moi)* determined by the other. More subtly, it separates two opposed ways of describing the relation of the *ego (moi)* or of *Dasein* to the other; and the difficulty consists in locating exactly where the line of division passes. I will attempt to show that the entire opposition turns on the possibility, or not, of a substitution. And we are all the more authorized to follow this hypothesis by the fact that Levinas himself—rather late, it is true, but nevertheless with great precision—commented upon this very paragraph from *Sein und Zeit*.[15]

After having determined the *In-der-Welt-sein* (chap. 2), then the worldliness of the world (chap. 3), in order to attain the *In-Sein* as such (chap. 5) and care (*Sorge*, chap. 6), to which everything leads, the transcendental analytic must along the way specify the *In-der-Welt-sein* as being-one's-self (*Selbst-sein*) and also as being-with *(Mitsein)* (chap. 4). In this context, the question of the other is posed, but so too is the question of the *They (das Man)*, as if alterity necessarily were in league with the indifferentiation of the self. Let's limit ourselves, for the moment, to underscoring that, for the analytic of *Dasein*, the existential of being-with *(Mitsein)* strictly implies the "other," that is to say the other as a(nother) *Dasein:* "On the basis of this *like-with* [*mithaften*] being-in-the-world, the world is always already the one that I share with the others. The world of Da-sein is a *with-world* [*Mitwelt*]. Being-in [*In-Sein*] is *being-with* [*Mitsein*] others. The innerworldly being-in-itself of others is *Mitda-sein* [or co-*Dasein*]."[16] Without any ambiguity, *Dasein*, precisely because it opens a world of itself (as *In-der-Welt-sein*), opens it as a world that from the outset is offered to alterity, as a co-world. Thus being in this co-world immediately implies being-with others, others who are themselves in the mode of *Dasein*. In short, *Dasein* implies, in its very being, co-*Dasein:* "Only because it has the essential structure of being-with, is one's own Da-sein *Mitda-sein* [or co-*Dasein*] as encounterable by others."[17] Thus, that *Dasein* implies an other *Dasein* (as another being) does not yet pose any difficulties. The difficulties begin only later, when the point is to determine how a *Dasein* encounters the other: does it go right away, simply as co-*Dasein*, to encounter the other?

If the other can be encountered only as a(nother) *Dasein*, it is properly necessary that it be encountered as a *Dasein*, and not as a being of the world that would not measure up to a *Dasein* (a *nichtdaseinsmässig* being). Thus it will be necessary for *Dasein* to relate to another otherwise than it would relate to an innerworldly being, which is to say, otherwise than through *Besorgen* (taking care) (of a task, or of a need), which only applies to an innerworldy being. Nevertheless, this mode of encounter cannot be called *Sorge* (care, *cura*) either, for *Sorge* will only intervene in view of the being-toward-death of *Dasein* proper. Thus *Dasein* can only relate to the other (as) *Dasein* in a particular mode, that of *Fürsorge* (solicitude, concern, care for . . .). Let us now describe the mode of access to the phenomenon of the

THE REASON OF THE GIFT

other (as) *Dasein*. First, a remark: the German *Fürsorge* indicates, taken in its first instance for a "faktische soziale Einrichtung," what French calls "assistance publique," and English "Medicare" (America) or "social care" (Britain).[18] A first meaning of this term inevitably follows: social assistance, *Fürsorge*, goes first and foremost, and most frequently, to occupy itself (in the mode of *Besorgen*) with innerworldly beings, of which an other (as) *Dasein* would happen to find himself deprived, and thus endeavors to provide such things for him as food, clothing, shelter, etc. Now, Heidegger condemns this *Fürsorge* as "deficient." One might be astonished, even scandalized, by this because the biblical care toward "the widow and the orphan" (for example, Exod. 22:21, Deut. 10:18, or Isa. 1:18) thus finds itself downgraded to the level of a deficient mode of *Fürsorge*. One's astonishment would be well justified, for even though *Fürsorge* cares for the other only indirectly and attends first of all directly to innerworldly beings, of which the other has urgent need *(besorgen)*, this first-response emergency assistance nonetheless remains the existential (and not only the existentiell) condition of possibility for other modes of *Fürsorge*.[19] This justice thus rendered to "sublime materialism,"[20] one must also recognize Heidegger's reasons for condemning its "deficiency": precisely because it is concentrated upon the first-response emergency goods, and thus those of first usage, this assistance in fact treats only innerworldly beings-at-hand *(Zuhandenes)* and thus *not* the other (as) *Dasein*. The other (as) *Dasein* thereby remains undifferentiated, non-individuated, even anonymous, such that the same assistance could be applied to anyone without distinction. Paradoxically—and thus the pertinence of Heidegger's analysis—the assistance (the *Fürsorge* as a *Besorgen* that is unaware of itself) does not concern itself with the alterity of the other (as) *Dasein*, because it does not even consider *Dasein*'s individualized otherness, identified as such and for itself. Assistance socializes alterity, which it thereby renders indeterminate and indifferent. The other becomes whomever and anyone; he thus takes on the faceless visage of *They (das Man)*, and in the end remains in a deficit of *alterity*.[21] Heidegger's argument thus situates itself, in effect, upon the conceptual field that will become Levinas's: the recognition of the other as the Other, without match or equal.

However it may be with this first "deficient" mode of *Für-sorge*, it allows by contrast a derivation of its positive mode or, more precisely, a glimpse of the "two extreme possibilities" of this positive mode.[22] The first possibility comes down to "tak[ing] the other's 'care' [*Sorge*] away from him and put[ting] itself in his place in taking care [*Besorgen*], [. . .] *leap[ing] in* for him [*für ihn einspringen*],"[23] thus unburdening him of his care *(Sorge)* by taking his place in the management of his material needs *(ses besoins en étants) (im Besorgen)*. This first mode is inadequate for the (one might say Hegelian) reason that Heidegger formulates unequivocally: such a *Dasein*, unburdened of its care *(Sorge)* by another *Dasein*, would immediately fall under its domination *(Herrschaft)*, even if silent or unconscious;[24] once again, the other would no longer be himself, but instead a servant of *Dasein* insofar as mine, and thus not yet properly another (as) *Dasein*. Thus, and specifically in order to respect the alterity of the other *Dasein* (and thus, doubtless, of the other himself), it is necessary to pass to the second "extreme possibility" of *Fürsorge*, "which does not so much leap in for [*nicht einspringt*] the other as *leap ahead* of him [*vorausspringt*], not in order to take 'care' [*Sorge*] away from him, but to [*sic*] first to give it back to him [*zurückzugeben*] as such."[25] For the first time, the assistance *(Fürsorge)* of *Dasein* as mine no longer concerns innerworldly beings, to which the other could attend *(Besorgen)*, but the other's existence (or potentiality-of-being) even as other, (as) *Dasein*. Solicitude *(Fürsorge)* finally becomes, literally, care for *(Sorge für)* the other as such, namely, as another *Dasein*. And this care for the other (as) *Dasein* consists precisely in *not* claiming to take his place, but instead in allowing him to take upon himself the weight of his own possibility, "the burden of being."[26] Care for the other amounts to *not substituting oneself for him*, and instead allowing him to carry his load, that of being, about which he cannot not decide, because it is what is most his own.[27] Care of the other requires abandoning him to him*self*.

III. THE SELF AS UNSUBSTITUTABLE

Heidegger thus maintains, within the frame of the analysis of *Mitsein* (§26), this strange paradox: that the solicitude that takes true care *(Fürsorge)* for the other consists precisely in *not* substituting for him. But on what argument, and thus through what description, is this paradox established? Obviously here the matter is not one of selfishness or indifference (which in any case are simple moral determinations, and thus ontic, lacking any existential pertinence), but instead of the strict ontological demand for a higher care for the other, which makes manifest that he, too, is defined by his care of self *(Sorge)*. In the end, the point is to recognize in the other the originary determination of *Dasein*: "Because its essence lies rather in the fact that it in each instance has to be its being as its own, the term Da-sein, as a pure expression of being, has been chosen to designate this being."[28] Thus, for *Dasein*, to accede to the self always means either enduring mineness or deviating from it: "Mineness [*Jemeinigkeit*] belongs to existing Da-sein as the condition of the possibility of authenticity [appropriation] and inauthenticity [in-appropriation]."[29]

Now, *Dasein* only accomplishes its ownmost—properly attaining to oneself and attaining what is proper to oneself by appropriating being, or rather, by allowing oneself to appropriate oneself through being—by exercising its final possibility, by being in the mode of being-*toward*-death.[30] Indeed, my possibility implies not only the possibility of my death but my death as possibility (of impossibility). Such a death, as possibility, implies that no one can excuse himself from it, and thus that no one can take up the task for me, nor substitute himself for me. Doubtless, someone else can "die in my place," through sacrifice or devotion to me (or another). However, even in such a case, the one who sacrifices himself first of all will die his own death and not mine; and, second, he will only spare me my death for a time, because in the end there will always come a moment in which I, in person, will have to live *my* death. No one will ever do that in my stead. "Death is a possibility of being that Da-sein always has to take upon itself," for *"No one can take the other's dying away from him."*[31] If I, *Dasein*, wish to attain my ownmost and my ipseity, I must never allow an other to substitute for me, especially at the instant of my death, "essentially and irreplaceably mine [*unvertretbar*]."[32] The complete definition of death "as the *ownmost nonrelational, certain [. . .] possibility,"*[33] is articulated according to this ownmost and, so to speak, follows from it, as first and only superlative. In death, as a possibility that I anticipate, what is at stake is my appropriation *(Eigentlichkeit)* to myself *(Selbstheit)* as *Dasein*. I am as I will die *(sum moribundus),*[34] alone, because unsubstitutable.

This conclusion is confirmed *a contrario* by the fact that substitution—for Heidegger does admit the possibility—always relates back to the *They (das Man)*, in its ceaselessly repeated attempt to disappropriate *Dasein* of itself, which is to say, to restore "a *constant tranquilization about death."*[35] Of course, the possibility of substitution belongs as a matter of principle to *Dasein* insofar as it is open to others;[36] but the substitution that follows always debases this *Dasein* in a public event, accessible to everyone and no one—in short, accessible to the *They:* "Dying, which is essentially and irreplaceably [*unvertretbar,* unsubstitutably] mine, is perverted into a publicly occurring event which the they encounters."[37] Substitution, whether it is for me by another, or for another by me, in every case prevents (in me or in the other) *Dasein*'s appropriation of itself.

Thus it becomes clear that, for Heidegger, substitution contradicts ipseity in every case (the other for me, or me for the other). I am *Dasein* only in the first person, and never through another, nor for another. As a consequence, *Fürsorge* must also always let itself fall back completely into *Sorge:* "Even if only privatively, care is always taking care of things [*Besorgen*] and concern [*Fürsorge,* solicitude]."[38] Even here, the *für-* remains a mere add-on prefix,[39] changing nothing in the center of gravity of the care that is *Sorge*. As the meaning of the being of *Dasein*, *Sorge* stays centered on *Dasein* as mine.[40]

IV. THE *ME* IN THE ACCUSATIVE

The conflict becomes completely clear. For Heidegger, ipseity excludes the substitution of the other for me, or me for the other, and is decided exclusively and solely by *my* anticipatory resoluteness regarding *my* death. For Levinas, "subjectivity is from the first substitution,"[41] and I only attain to my ipseity by substituting for the other or by allowing the other to substitute for me—for *here* the one comes back precisely to the other, if at least one of us, *I (moi)*, comes back to the other and not to the self. "The fact of not evading the burden imposed by the suffering of others defines ipseity itself."[42] The justification for this reversal remains to be made, and will be accomplished in several steps.

The first step leads to rejecting the claim that ipseity can be attained on the basis of the sole *I*, understood as *Dasein*—the sole *I*, which is also to say, the *I* as solitary. Now, subjectivity is not summed up by the supposedly transparent relationship of consciousness to itself, because "consciousness, knowing of oneself by oneself, is not all there is to the notion of subjectivity."[43] Of course, this does not mean that subjectivity retreats into the unconscious, but that the circle in which the *cogitatio* is closed never allows access to what, in the *ego*, specifies it most radically as in itself. And the same impossibility exists for the *cogitatio*'s other privileged modality, the will: "The ego [*Moi*] [. . .] is this original expiation. This expiation is involuntary, for it is prior to the will's initiative (prior to the origin)."[44] I once again underscore that what Levinas does not hesitate to call an " 'inversion' of intentionality," which would go "against intentionality,"[45] implies nothing less than a wholesale "inversion of consciousness," which becomes a "consciousness countercurrentwise."[46] Far from the *ego* attaining itself and experiencing itself by returning upon itself, it will reach itself only by going against the current that comes upon it from elsewhere. Thus, just as Levinas retains from Descartes the idea of the infinite, so does he reject the *cogito* (at least according to its standard formulation),[47] for an important reason: while the *ego* of the *cogito* decides itself for itself through a thinking that is centrifugal, but which always returns upon itself, the *ego* of the idea of the infinite discovers itself preceded by what will always remain exterior to it, the infinite itself, and which nevertheless defines the *ego* always more originally than does the *ego* itself. If one can still speak here of subjectivity, it cannot any more name itself than it can conceive itself. As a subjectivity without an *I*, without a name established in the nominative, it no longer carries any name other than that attributed to it from outside, as a sobriquet: *me* [*moi*]. Me, or the name that comes from elsewhere, which names me from the very place where the other sees me, as I will never see myself. Me, or the name that names me as I never will.

Henceforward, I name myself "in the accusative form, which is a modification of no nominative form."[48] I have no proper name, because even my me is "not an ego [*Moi*], but me under assignation"[49]—but which assignation, and by what? Clearly, my assignation by that which accuses me, I who have a "*self*, from the first in the accusative form (or under accusation!)."[50] It is necessary here to keep something of a phenomenological meaning associated with accusation, beyond its patent juridical meaning: I know myself as an accused *me*, as when a light that is too bright shines at me and *singles out (accuse)* my features, rendering them more visible to my spectator, without my being able either to see them or to control them. Under luminous accusation, I no longer phenomenalize myself from my point of view, but rather from that of the other. I become me in a light from elsewhere. And here, I am seen without seeing (myself); I do not appear first through myself and for myself (as if my phenomenality could produce itself beginning from myself), but instead, I first and in fact only *appear summoned before* the other; against both common sense and the juridical situation, I do not appear first, and in order, then, to *appear summoned before* the other; instead, I only appear if I *appear summoned before* or in front of . . . [the other].[51]

Now there comes a second step: identifying or at least desig-

nating that which accuses or points out, even if only in the phenomenological sense, the elsewhere from which the other, also
come from elsewhere, summons me to appear *(comparaître)*; in
short, that in relation to which (or to whom) I discover myself in
this situation where one names me in the accusative. One could
limit oneself to a simple, juridical response: I am named in the
accusative *me* because an other, eventual holder of the role of
the other in general, accuses me with a certain charge *(crimen)*.
But this explanation doesn't hold, first because it only works by
arbitrarily presupposing my guilt, as if it were always already
the case that I am guilty; it assumes that accusation is immediately equivalent to indictment, and thus that the accusative first
derives from morality, from the determination between good and
evil. Now, it could be that the Levinassian accusative (as much
as the Heideggerian *Gewissen*) must, at least here, be understood
once again in the extra-moral sense, which is to say in the strictly
phenomenal sense. Next, and above all, the juridical explanation
of the *me (moi)* seems to grant that I *would be*, first and to begin
with, the me through or by myself, such that it could only receive
the charge of accusation afterward; thus my existence as *I* would
again precede my qualification as *me*, if only because it renders
it possible; thus the accusative would leave the *ego* intact in its
unassailed nominative, confirming it by indicting it. But here it is
precisely the point to think a *me* that is anterior to the *I*, a *me* that
dispenses absolutely with the *I* and has never assumed its form.
In short, the point is to think a *me* outside of being: "Not strictly
speaking an ego [*moi*] set up in the nominative in its identity, but
first constrained to. . . . It is set up as it were in the accusative
form."[52] The *me*, thus taken back *(repris)*, is not declined as the
object case of a nominative *I*. On the contrary, this *I* would be
declined instead from a sole and originary *me* (accusative), in its
essentially adversative character, considered from elsewhere; the
I would only appear by neutralizing, after the fact, the anarchy
prior to the *me*. Prior, indeed, because the accusation does not
make a ground upon some thing (a being), which would precede
it and, supporting itself on it, eventually resist the accusation, or

exonerate or *exculpate* itself from the accusation. Now, it is not enough that one accuse me for me to discover myself originally as a *me* in the accusative; on the contrary, the posture of the accused, if limited to a solely *moral* horizon, presupposes again and always my *ontic* self-sufficiency, precedence, and independence. Again, it grants me the status of a being, in order to assure me evermore of *being* and to appropriate me thus to myself as subject, even if only to be able later to accuse me as a moral or juridical subject. Finally, accusation, even understood in the extra-moral sense, no longer allows for the anteriority of the other over me, nor therefore the *me* itself, because accusation can allow itself to be reduced to a call of *my* conscience, by itself, in the sense where, according to the existential analytic, "Dasein is at the same time the caller and the one summoned," such that it "calls itself."[53] At fault, conscience remains no less autistic (the ethical autism of the scrupulous), because one can very well find fault with oneself, without any access to the other. And most often, such is the case. Thus, it is necessary to refrain from thinking the accusative on the basis of moral accusation, or even the call (of conscience), lest one paradoxically reinforce the ontic primacy of an implicit nominative and, in so doing, the *ego* of metaphysics.

Thus we arrive at the third and final moment. How can one manage to radicalize the accusative that must constitute me without presupposing any subject prior to the accusation? We have stated it: by not making the accusative contingent upon a fault committed by an *I* that is prior. Doubtless, but am I not, in one way or another, always already guilty of a fault that I committed, and thus am I not always already being before that fault, by being an *I* in the nominative? Will it be necessary to renounce allowing myself to be named "at the outset" in the accusative, which is to say, before any accusation? Not at all, for there remains a way: the accusative can exert itself in an incontestably extra-moral mode, that is to say, one that does not imply that *I* be responsible in the mode of an ontic precedent. Now, for this path to become apparent, it is necessary to construct a crucial experiment in accordance with the principle that "to be oneself, the state of

THE REASON OF THE GIFT

being a hostage, is always to have one *degree* of responsibility *more*, the responsibility for the responsibility of the other."[54] Let us be precise: at issue here is not a responsibility in addition to a first responsibility, but a degree more in the fact of responsibility; put another way, a responsibility raised to a higher power, a responsibility squared (R^2). What responsibility squared can I shoulder, if not precisely a responsibility without any prior fault, without reason, counter to the principle of sufficient reason, and to which I no longer have to answer in conformity to a law or a norm? Namely, the responsibility to let *myself* be named responsible not for what I would have committed as an *I* (a pre-being) in the role of efficient cause, but for what I *have not* committed and, by definition, for that of which I cannot assume the cause, namely for what the *other* has committed: "being responsible for his brother right up to being responsible for his freedom."[55] But, this result poses a new question: how can I know for certain what the other has committed, without fantasizing or dreaming up a morbid culpability? In order to do this, it would be necessary to know with certainty what only another than I can have committed, and which I, in no case, would have committed, even if I had wanted to: what I would in no case be able to will. Now, this act, which I by definition can neither want nor be able to do (and which is excepted from the principle of sufficient reason) can be identified without difficulty: it is my persecution by the other, the persecution that he would exercise against me, "the unlimited accusative of persecution."[56] Paradoxically, but inevitably, responsibility squared, taken in its extra-moral sense, will be a third stage, truly "a degree [. . .] more." Not responsibility in the first sense (responsibility for what *I* have done), nor in the second (responsibility for what the *other* has done), but truly in the third sense: responsibility for what the other has committed *against me*, and which certainly imposes itself as originating elsewhere than in me, since the other committed it precisely *against me*. Such a "responsibility of the ego for what the ego has not wished," which is deepened in "responsibility for the responsibility of the other,"[57] this is what unquestionably constitutes me as a *me*, precisely because it is unfolded without the will,[58] without any prior being,[59] in short without me, or rather without *I* and prior to me. Only this responsibility to a "degree more" and in a decidedly extra-moral sense invests me definitively in the accusative, as an originary *me*, which is to say without *ego: "under* accusation by everyone, the responsibility for everyone goes to the point of substitution. A subject is a hostage."[60] The hostage, or the *me* without self, at the mercy of the one who accuses.

The violence of the term "hostage" requires that we pay close attention. "Subjectivity as hostage"[61]—certainly, the formula signifies that my exposition to the other does not depend on me, because it precedes me and institutes me by derivation from him. But above all it signifies that my subjectivity does not depend on the other, either, at least not on the other understood according to a relation that would unite me to him as to another being: "Through substitution for others, the oneself escapes *relations.*"[62] Between him and me, there is nothing in common, no third party, no mediator, not even a relation, only the pure "possibility of putting oneself in the place of the other," which precedes sympathy or respect, because it alone makes them possible. "Hostage" does not define a condition (that would stabilize me on my foundations), but a *non*-condition, an instability that thus installs me, by derivation, in the situation of ethical becoming: "The non-condition of being hostage [*L'incondition d'otage*] is not the limit case of solidarity, but the condition for all solidarity."[63] In other words, the hostage (along with the substitution that elicits the hostage) does not arise from ethics, but establishes its conditions of possibility. Substitution does not belong to ethics, but exercises in relation to it a transcendental function: it renders it possible. The hostage, who discovers himself responsible for everyone and for everything that they have done (to me), has nevertheless not committed any fault (he is responsible, not guilty), and he is phenomenalized in the accusative without anyone accusing him of anything (or condemning him). But, without any fault or condemnation, he thus attains his only possible ipseity: "The ipseity, in the passivity without arche characteristic of identity, is a hostage. The word *I* means *here I am*, answering for everything and for everyone."[64] Answering for what I have not done—this defines the condition of those who have survived extermination, for all feel the duty (the responsibility) to be responsible for what has happened *against them*, and above all *against those who were annihilated*. The obligation to answer for it signifies a duty to speak in their name and to speak against those who did the annihilating: responsibility to respond to the unthinkable, for speech to respond to the unsayable. The deportees and the zeks [Gulag inmates], when they return, speak nothing other than this charge to stigmatize evil, which weighs upon their innocence.

Thus substitution belongs neither to moral philosophy nor to ethics, because it accomplishes ipseity in a nonmetaphysical and non-ontological mode.

V. ELECTION OF THE HOSTAGE

Thus substitution asserts itself as the culmination of individuation and of ipseity, precisely by means of the heteronomy that it demands, and that it *dispenses*. Following in the wake of Heidegger, but also of Sartre, Levinas never gave up on the question of the self and of its mode of being (or of nonbeing), which engaged him from the beginning; but in the end, his answer contradicted in every way both Heidegger and Sartre: the individuation of the self does not pass through the *I*, its for-itself *(pour-soi)*, nor its mineness *(Jemeinigkeit)*, and in particular not through my possibility, as *Dasein*, of being-toward-*my*-death; my individuation, on the contrary, proceeds from my responsibility toward the other, before every accusation and every response, which is to say, from my absolutely unconditioned responsibility, without reason or cause. And this ipseity—contradictory, without reason—thus no longer belongs to metaphysics, whose two principles it contradicts.

So the other accuses me, but first of all in the sense in which, by highlighting *(en accusant)* the features of a face, one makes it clearer and easier to recognize. The other accuses me in the accusative, such that he places me for the first time in the light, gives me the depth of a face that I would not have without the light of his gaze, and shows me as myself (including to myself). I become myself and unique precisely insofar as the other summons me, thus "accused as unique."[65] What makes me me does not coincide with what I think, nor with what I think of it, nor with what I wish, nor even with what I am—here thinking remains as "indeterminate" as being—but with that for which and *to whom* I answer. "I am 'in myself' through the others."[66] We should even say that this exteriority or deportation of the *me* outside of itself works its paradox as a sort of phenomenological reduction. Because the issue is that of attaining an "ipseity *reduced* to the irreplaceable,"[67] we must then ask: What is in me such that nothing can substitute for it and replace me? It is neither my thought, which can always be replaced by another, nor my resolution to be or not to be according to my final possibility, which can always be denied, but only my responsibility. My responsibility raised to the point of substitution confirms itself to be the only irreducible in this new reduction. Not in the sense of that for which I would become responsible through my (moral) decision, always subsequent to the (ontic) *I*, but in the sense of that for which I discover myself responsible without having either willed it or thought it, because it is the others who have in advance made me a hostage of their own responsibilities. I thus find myself, strangely by dint of substitution and in its favor, the "non-*interchangeable* par excellence,"[68] because "nothing is unique, that is, *refractory* to concepts, except the I of responsibility."[69] Indeed, I become irreducibly myself, or put another way, I identify myself with that which resists every reduction of the *me* when I accomplish this perfect *residuum*—not taking up the variations and intermittences of the *I* (even understood as *Dasein*), but the *fait accompli* of my responsibility for that which does not depend on me, never has depended on me and never will—the responsibilities that others have taken without me but *for* me. For me: not in my favor, but in my place and on my account.

THE REASON OF THE GIFT

This fact, accomplished before me and for me, qualifies me with an unequaled facticity.

Now we catch a better glimpse of the power of the re-reading (in the double sense of a recuperation and a correction) that Levinas carried out on the doctrine of the *Selbstheit* elaborated in *Sein und Zeit*. Where the *Dasein* reigns in the first person, the *me* in the accusative suddenly appears; where resoluteness decides and wills, the hostage undergoes a decision that he had not made; where *Dasein* anticipates its possibility, the substitute knows himself to be thrown into what it is no longer possible for him to avoid. But above all, where *Dasein* manages to individualize itself by itself, and thus to arrive at self-steadfastness or self-constancy *(Selbst-ständigkeit)*, precisely because "the *constancy of the self* means nothing other than anticipatory resoluteness,"[70] the hostage only attains the "superindividuation of the ego"[71] (an individuation "to the power"), by entrusting himself to the other, for "the uniqueness of the self is the very fact of bearing the fault of another."[72] Or, what amounts to the same thing, "God loves man as an ipseity."[73]

In fact, when Levinas himself commented upon *Sein und Zeit* section 26, he concluded his objection with these words: "This would be the *I* of the one who is chosen to answer for his fellowman and is *thus* identical to itself, and *thus* the self. A uniqueness of chosenness!"[74] It is necessary to go that far: if I am insofar as a hostage, this is because I discover myself always already chosen. There is a "Here I am" even in the "You!" of the one who condemns me. The condition of the hostage, provided that one does not too quickly understand it in the moral sense, indicates, exactly as election, that I am only myself on the basis of the *me* signified to me by the other. I am not the signification that the other would impose upon me, yet the other nevertheless does indeed signify to *me* who I am.

Still, other questions remain: might not the "I, unique and chosen,"[75] who knows himself only insofar as the other gives him his signification, correspond to the *adonné* (the gifted), which receives itself from what it receives? Could this be an ethical version of the *adonné*? Not at all, because what is at issue through and through, as we have seen, is an intrigue in the extra-moral sense, one of strict phenomenology. Does Heidegger's *Jemeinigkeit* truly signify the possession of its being by the *I*? As if what revealed itself as mine would be that which was claimed by an *I*? Instead, isn't it a matter of the burden of a decision regarding being, which falls as a responsibility on a *me (moi)*? And, in this case, would not *Dasein* also (and first of all) become a hostage— the hostage of being?

These questions thus remain. But this itself proves that, between Heidegger and Levinas, what is at issue is a combat between two types of thought.

FOUR

Sketch of a Phenomenological Concept of Sacrifice

I. THE APORIA OF SACRIFICE

Strictly speaking, we should not begin with sacrifice, at least in the sense of a noun, or of a substantive, because sacrifice *(sacrificium)* always results from the action of a verb, of the verb "to make" *(sacrum facere)*: a sacrifice appears once an agent has rendered something sacred, has set it apart from the profane and thereby consecrated it. Moreover, *sacrum facere* gave us *sacrifiement* in Old French, which states more clearly the process of rendering something sacred than the result of this process. The question of sacrifice concerns, then, first and above all the act of making something sacred and of wresting it from the profane (the act opposed to that of profanation), an act of which sacrifice is only a result that it limits itself to recording, without explaining it. This clarification nevertheless raises a difficulty: how can we conceive the transition between two terms, the profane and the sacred, while their very distinction becomes, in the epoch of nihilism in which we live, indistinct and confused, if not completely obscured? It is as if the "death of God," and above all what has provoked it—the realization that the highest values consist only in the valuation that confirms them, and thus are only worth what our valuations are worth—have abolished any difference between the sacred and the profane, and thereby any possibility of crossing over it by a *sacrifiement* (or on the contrary, by a profanation). Would not sacrifice disappear along with the sacred that is disappearing?

However, this is not the whole story. We still have a common, if not entirely vernacular, sense of sacrifice: sacrificing is equivalent to destroying; or, more precisely, to destroying what should not be destroyed, at least according to the normal practices of daily life, namely, the useful and the functional. In effect, beings understood as that which I make use of (*zuhanden* beings in Heidegger's distinction) are defined by the finality that links them not only to other ready-to-hand beings but ultimately to my own intention, which gathers the subordinated finalities of these beings into a network of finalities, all oriented toward myself as the center of a surrounding world. This being, not only useful but ready-to-hand (*usuel, zuhanden*), refers to me, and, in so doing, becomes for me my own world: it is good insofar as it is mine, it is a good insofar as it is my good. As a result, doing away with it would amount to my doing away with myself; and if, taking a step further in the negation, I were to destroy it, then I would also destroy myself. Such destruction of property as such, and even as my property—thus this destruction of myself—has not disappeared in our own time, and is still designated as sacrifice. Even daily, we are subject to its paroxysm in the form of *terrorism*. Both common usage and the media rely on the semantics of sacrifice in order to qualify terrorist acts: the terrorist, it is said, *sacrifices himself* for his cause, or else, he *sacrifices* the lives of his random victims in order to draw attention to this very cause. Such terms, as approximate and thus misleading as they may be, nevertheless retain some relevance because pure violence, without any moral or even political justification, in its stupidity and its barbarism, in fact elicits a paralyzing dread before an act that in principle is alien to the world of living beings or the community of reasonable people and obeys the logic, absurd to us, of another world which moreover denies and annihilates our own. Terrorism abolishes property, innocent people, and the terrorist himself, because it accomplishes first and radically the destruction of all beings as useful and functional, and the destruction for us of the organization of the world itself in terms of ends and accomplishment. Thus destroyed, the everyday thing (*l'usuel*) becomes the sacred insofar as it no longer belongs to the world in which we can live, and in which it is our purpose or intention to live in the normality of the profane. Now, if we grant that terror under its polymorphous though faceless figures remains today our ultimate experience of the sacred, and that this figure of the sacred, as debased as it proves to be, nevertheless allows us a common concept of sacrifice, then what makes a profane thing sacred, the *sacrifiement*, consists in its destruction. The terrorist produces the sacred (under the figure of absurd horror) by *destroying* life, including his own.[1] The process that makes the profane sacred entails the destruction of the thing thus sacrificed.[2] One access to sacrifice thus remains available to us to the extent that the experience of terrorism guarantees us the experience of the destruction of property as such, and thus of the world as ours.

Nevertheless, this first result, by providing us an indisputable because perfectly negative access to the sacred and to the *sacrifiement*, only reinforces the aporia. For the point is not merely to deplore the fact that destruction is the only remaining figure of sacrifice today, but above all to ascertain the extent to which, even in this form, its intelligibility remains problematic. How, indeed, does destroying something contribute to making it sacred? What does sacrifice do if all it does is undo? What can it consecrate if it limits itself to annihilating? To what or to whom can it give, since it nullifies the content of any gift and nullifies itself as possible giver? The definition of sacrifice as the destruction of a good as such not only explains nothing of sacrifice but could actually explain its opposite—the self-appropriation of autarchy. Indeed, the wise and the strong want to rid themselves of a possession by destroying it and thereby becoming free of it; they alone can do this and they prove it to themselves by surviving what they destroy in themselves: in making a sacrifice of other goods (by ascesis, renunciation, mutilation, and so forth), they demonstrate their autarchy to others; or rather they prove at least to themselves their autonomy and ataraxy. Sacrifice thus becomes the auto-celebration of the ascetic ideal, in which the *ego* attains a kind of *causa sui* by no longer owing anything to anyone, not even its own person to the world. Sacrifice, understood as the destruction of a good, can be inverted into a construction of the self, which sacrifices nothing of its own, only the world to itself.

II. SACRIFICE ACCORDING TO EXCHANGE

Thus we must give up on defining sacrifice only by the destruction of a possession. In fact, it becomes possible to speak of sacrifice only if one introduces a third term, beyond the destroyer and the good destroyed—precisely the third, the other. Even in the most banal understanding of sacrifice, for example the sacrifice of a pawn or a piece in chess, the other already appears, even if only in the most basic guise of the mimetic rival, the alter ego, my opponent: even if, in making this supposed gift to my opponent, my purpose is simply to strengthen *my* position, it is my position vis-à-vis *him*, and I sacrifice this piece *to him*. In short, my sacrifice always assumes the other as its horizon of possibility. Thus it is the other that determines the destruction of a good, either because he benefits from it as its new recipient (I transfer it to him while mourning its loss), or because he shares its loss with me as my rival (I give it up in order to deprive him of it, in order to strengthen my position).

In this new sense, where it occurs within the horizon of the other, does sacrifice become more intelligible than in the previous case, where it is pure and simple destruction of a good? Undoubtedly, because we notice immediately that it is in fact no longer simply a matter of destruction, but also of privation (with destruction, but also sometimes without). And this obtains on both sides of the alternative. On the one hand, I deprive myself of a good, because I can do without it, and in this way assure my autonomy (autarchy, ataraxy, etc.); in other words, I deprive myself of a good precisely in order to prove to myself that it has only a minor importance and that I remain myself even without it; hence by losing a possession that is other than me, I gain a more perfect possession of myself. On the other hand, I deprive myself

THE REASON OF THE GIFT

of a good, not because I would simply destroy it, but because by destroying it or by making it unavailable to me, I want to divest myself of it to the point that, by this definitive loss, another might possibly appropriate it in my stead; in fact, I display this good I have renounced so that it may become available for the other to appropriate it. Nevertheless, these two situations clearly differ. In the first case, it is indeed enough for me to deprive myself of a good (to the extent that I myself survive), in order to prove its dispensable character and in this way demonstrate my autarchy: the sacrifice is accomplished perfectly by itself. The second case is rather different: admittedly, I manage to deprive myself of a good (I indeed sacrifice it) but this renunciation is not *as such* sufficient for some other to take possession of that of which I have nevertheless deprived myself; the sacrifice remains unfinished: my renunciation only allowed for the display of the good, which, though made available, still remains in escheat at this point in the process: less given than just given up. For even when I divest myself of a good, whether or not the other takes possession of it is not up to me; that depends only on the other. By my decision alone, the sacrifice can thus only be accomplished halfway; its realization does not derive from my simple act of dispossession, but awaits the other's acceptance, and thus depends upon another decision, on an *other* decision, come from elsewhere. I can at best act *as if* my dispossession were equivalent to a taking possession by the other, but I can neither assure that nor assume it. Dispossession cannot anticipate reception because the other's acceptance can come only from the other himself, and thus by definition escapes me. Sacrifice involves my dispossession, but my dispossession is not enough for a sacrifice, which only acceptance by the other can ratify. If we assume that giving up is enough to begin the sacrifice, accomplishing it as a gift is contingent upon its acceptance by the other. There is nothing optional or secondary about this discrepancy which defines and marks the irreducible distance between me and the other, such that neither I nor the other can abolish it. Even when offered (or rather: precisely *because* offered), it is part of the definition of sacrifice that it can nevertheless be refused and disdained by the other—in this specifically lies the other's role. Thus, even if defined within the horizon of the other, the destruction or disappropriation of a good is not enough to account fully for the possibility of sacrifice.

Yet it happens that the most current explanation of sacrifice, produced by sociology and the sociology of religion in particular, presupposes exactly the opposite: that my dispossession of a good is enough for the effective accomplishment of a sacrifice. Sacrifice would consist in effecting the loss of a good (by destruction or by devolution) for the benefit of an other (divine or mortal, most often superior hierarchically), such that he accepts it and consequently renders a counter-gift to the one who initiated the sacrifice—with this reciprocity constituting the decisive presupposition. Obviously, the realization of the sacrifice by its initiator does not imply and does not at all guarantee the acceptance of the good that has been ceded, and still less, the reciprocity of a counter-gift. Nevertheless, this interpretation of sacrifice imposes itself, perpetuates itself, and prevails, even today. How does it manage to do so? By assuming what it cannot prove, to wit, that the acceptance and the counter-gift always (or at least in the majority of cases, as the standard situation) follow from the dispossession (with or without destruction). But, once again, how does this presupposition legitimate itself? By implicitly basing the entire explanation of sacrifice on the model of exchange.[3] Moreover, in the majority of cases, we find the three terms gift, exchange, and sacrifice equated, or even substituted without distinction for one another. Just as the gift consists in giving up a possession in order to obligate the other to give back a counter-gift (*do ut des*), and just as exchange implies that every good that passes from the one to the other is compensated by a good (or a sum of money) passing from the other to the one, in like fashion, the sacrificer (the sacrificing agent) abandons a good (by dispossession, of exposure or destruction), so that the supposedly superior other (divine or mortal) will accept it, and in so doing, enter into a contractual relation, and, by contract, return a good (real

THE REASON OF THE GIFT

or symbolic). In the three cases, under the imprecise (and confused) names of gift, exchange, and sacrifice, the same economy of contract obtains: I bind myself to you by abandoning a possession, *therefore* you bind yourself to me by accepting it, *therefore* you owe me an equivalent item in return. Henceforth, sacrifice does not destroy any more than the gift gives up, because both work to establish exchange; or rather, where sacrifice destroys and the gift cedes, both operate thereby to establish the economy of reciprocity.

We must conclude that destruction or dispossession and the horizon of the other still do not allow us to determine a concept of sacrifice, but only lead us to assimilate it with exchange in the same confusion that undermines the notion of the gift. In this context, at best, one would call sacrifice the imprudence of an incomplete exchange where a gift is given up without knowing whether an acceptance will ratify it, while at worst, sacrifice would be the illusion of a contractual arrangement that no one would ever have entered into with the one who is making the sacrifice. Unless it were a matter of simple deception, of the other or of oneself, claiming to give up unconditionally, hoping all the while, secretly or unconsciously, to receive a hundredfold what one loses only once. It would be better instead to consider the very term sacrifice an impropriety, an empty or contradictory concept, and apply to sacrifice the contradiction that Derrida deplored in the gift: "The truth of the gift [. . .] suffices to annul the gift. The truth of the gift is equivalent to the non-gift or to the non-truth of the gift."[4] We can thus say that the truth of sacrifice culminates in exchange, that is to say, in the non-truth of sacrifice, since it should consist precisely of a relinquishing without return; it also ends in the truth of the non-gift par excellence, that is to say, the confirmation that whenever one believes he speaks of, and makes, a sacrifice, one still hopes for an exchange and a return that would be all the more profitable, since one claimed to have lost everything.

III. THE MISUNDERSTANDING OF THE GIFT

Nevertheless, a way could be opened through the aporia itself, and thanks to it. More precisely, the extension of the aporia of the gift to sacrifice might already indicate another path—by making us think sacrifice precisely in its relation to the gift. We would then no longer only think of it as the dispossession (yea the destruction) of a good within the horizon of the other, but also as a moment of the more comprehensive phenomenon of the gift. For the phenomenon of the gift at the outset manifests much more than exchange: as we have attempted to demonstrate elsewhere, the gift can and thus must be separated from exchange, by letting its natural meaning reduce to givenness. For, while the economy (of exchange) denatures the gift, if reduced to givenness, the gift excepts itself from the economy, by freeing itself from the rules of exchange. The gift in effect proves able to accomplish itself, even and especially, by reducing each of the terms of exchange: without a giver *(donateur)*, or indeed without a recipient *(donataire)*— thus freeing itself without reciprocity—and even without a thing given—thus freeing itself from a logic of equality.[5] As reduced to the givenness in it, the gift is accomplished in an unconditioned immanence, which not only owes nothing to exchange, but dissolves its conditions of possibility. The gift so reduced performs itself with an *unconditioned* freedom—it never lacks anything that would prohibit it from giving itself, because, even without invoking the terms of the exchange, it still shows itself, even all the more so. But if the gift proves *unconditioned* in this way, would it not offer sacrifice its most appropriate site, since sacrifice claims precisely (though without at this juncture justifying its claim) to give and to give up *without condition?* In this hypothesis, the solution to the aporia of sacrifice would come from the answer to the aporia of the gift—from the reduction of the gift to givenness. We will need then to proceed to a reduction of sacrifice to givenness in order to formulate sacrifice, as one of its moments, in terms of the phenomenon of the reduced gift.

Where, then, does the most evident aporia arise when the

phenomenon of a gift unfolds? Precisely at the moment when the given gift *appears*. For when what the giver gives (a thing, a being, a piece of information [*une donnée*], a present, etc.) comes into full light, the gift as such inevitably starts to become obscured, and then to disappear. Indeed, the gift given, which takes on the consistency of the thing and of a being, occupies the center of the phenomenal stage, so as to conceal or even exclude everything else. Everything else, that is to say first of all the giver: for the giver disappears in his own gift: on the one hand, he must indeed give *something*, whatever may be the actual status of this something (a simple sign of good will or a real gift in itself, useful or useless, precious or trivial, inaugural or reciprocal, etc.); otherwise he would not appear at all as a giver giving. But, precisely to the extent that he gives his gift truly and irrevocably, the giver allows his given gift to separate itself from him, and assert itself as such, autonomous and thus available to the recipient, who appropriates it. The gift not only becomes a phenomenon independent of the phenomenon of the giver, but it excludes him, either by consigning him to the phenomenal background, or by obscuring him completely. This disappearance of the giver does not result from any recalcitrance on the part of the recipient, but from the very definition of the gift given; it is not ingratitude that causes the exclusion of the giver, yet this exclusion ultimately results by virtue of the very phenomenality of the gift given, in itself exclusive and appropriating. The giver must disappear (or at least his obviousness [*évidence*] must diminish and his presence withdraw) in order for the gift given to appear (or at least for its presence [*évidence*] to increase and for it to announce itself in the foreground). Otherwise, the gift given would not only not appear as such; it would not be truly given at all: its recipient would not dare to approach it or to extend his hand, or even to claim himself the recipient, because the tutelary and overhanging presence of the giver would still cast a shadow of possession over it. The recipient cannot take the gift given for his own, so long as he still *sees* in it the face and the power of its previous owner. The owner must withdraw from the giver, so that the gift can start to appear as given; but ultimately, the giver must disappear completely for the gift to appear as given definitively, that is to say, given up, abandoned.

And there is more. In effect, just as the gift appears only if the giver disappears, the gift thus abandoned ends by masking in itself not only the giver but the very process of the gift. If a gift appears as truly given only from the moment the giver yields it, the abandoning is reversed: the gift given appears because *it*, in turn, abandons its giver. But a gift without relation to any giver no longer bears the mark of any process of givenness, and thus appears as alien to what is given in it. Paradoxically, a gift truly given disappears as given, too. It appears henceforth only as a *found* object: a thing, a being or an object, which is found there, in front of me, by chance and without reason, such that I may wonder what status I should grant it: is it here in its own right (like a piece of fruit fallen from a tree), by the voluntary intention of an other (like an installation in a museum, a sign at the edge of the road, etc.), by involuntary accident (like a possession lost by its distracted owner, or stolen from him), or even possibly placed here by an anonymous giver, either for the benefit of some unspecified beneficiary (like the emergency phones on the side of a freeway), or for the benefit of an identified recipient, in which case it could be intended for an other, or for me? The gift-character of the found object is thus no longer self-evident; it is only one hypothesis among others, and not the least plausible. In the extreme, if my hermeneutic does not allow me (or does not wish) to recognize the gift as given, the gift as such disappears completely. What is specific to the gift—once we grant that it implies relinquishment in order to appear—thus consists in disappearing as given, and in allowing nothing more to appear than the neutral and anonymous presence, left without any origin, of a thing, of a being, or of an object, coming only from itself, never from elsewhere—nor originating from a giver or from a process of giving. The major aporia of the gift derives from this paradox: the gift given can appear only by erasing in its phenomenon its giver, the process of its gift, and, ultimately, its entire gift-character.

Two examples unambiguously confirm this paradox. First, the one in which Saint Augustine analyses the case of "a fiancé who gives a ring to his betrothed; but she loves the ring thus received more than the fiancé who gave it to her. Wouldn't we consider her adulterous in the very gift made to her by her fiancé, even while she loves what her fiancé has given her? Certainly, she loved what her fiancé gave her, but if she were to say: 'This ring is enough for me, now I don't want to see his face again,' what would she be? Who would not detest this lunacy? Who would not accuse her of adultery? You love gold instead of your husband, you love the ring instead of your fiancé; if you truly have in mind to love the ring in place of your fiancé and have no intention of seeing him, the deposit that he gave you as the token of his love would become the sign of your loathing."[6] Of course, in the case of this caricatured ingratitude, the issue for the theologian is to condemn the sin in general, as the attitude that leads us to love the gifts of God while rejecting God himself, who gives them to us. But the phenomenological description of the gift remains no less pertinent here: the betrothed first sees the fiancé, the giver, then the gift, the ring; the fiancé intended of course that, by seeing the gift (the ring), the betrothed would not stop seeing his face, the face of the giver. He reckoned to benefit from a phenomenal structure of reference (*Hinweis*): the phenomenon of the ring offering its own visibility and, moreover, conferring it to the (absent) visibility of the giver, who, by this indication, would benefit from a second-degree visibility, by association. In this way, the giver, invisible as such, gives being to the visible gift, but in return the visible gift gives him a visibility by proxy. Yet this exchange (the gift of being for the given exchanged for the gift of appearing for the giver) is not phenomenally valid: in fact, the betrothed sees and wants to see only the ring, and not, by indication and reference, the *facies sponsi*, the face of the giver. The gift given, as such and at the outset (the ring), monopolizes all of the visibility and condemns the giver to disappear from the visible stage. Henceforth, not only does the fiancé/giver no longer enter the phenomenon of the gift, but the gift-character of the given is erased: the ring becomes the possession of the betrothed, who sees nothing more than herself in it, possessing it. Along with the giver, the gift itself disappears.

In an entirely different context, but along the same descriptive line, and in describing the *es gibt*, such that it determines the appearance of time and being (for neither one nor the other *are*, so that with respect to them it is necessary to say *es gibt, it gives*), Heidegger insists on the phenomenal characteristic of the gift, which gives (itself) in this *it gives:* "The latter [*es gibt*] withdraws in favor of the gift [*zugünsten der Gabe*] which It gives [. . .]. A giving [*Geben*] which gives only its gift [*nur seine Gabe gibt*], but in the giving holds itself back and withdraws [*zurückhält und entzieht*], such a giving we call sending [*das Schicken*]."[7] We understand that the giving can precisely *not* give *itself*, more exactly *cannot* give *itself* in person, precisely because it gives its gift (the gift given), makes it appear as such, and in order to arrive at this, must not only remain in the background but must withdraw itself from visibility. The *es gibt*, because it gives (and dispenses) being as much as time, neither can nor should give itself. The giv*ing* gives only the giv*en*, it never gives *itself*. The giving cannot return on itself in a *donum sui*, as *causa sui* in metaphysics claims to do. Can we advance in the understanding of this fundamental impossibility? Possibly, by considering difference as such, namely, the difference that Heidegger in this case no longer calls ontological (*ontologische Differenz*), but the different from the same, the differentiation (*der Unterschieden aus dem Selben*, *der Unter-Schied*). What differs here is called the unique *Austrag*, the accord, which unfolds at once as being and as a being, which are both given in the same gesture, but precisely not in a similar posture: "Being shows itself as the unconcealing coming-over [*zeigt sich als die entbergende Überkommnis*]. Beings as such appear in the manner of the arrival that keeps itself concealed in uncon-cealedness [*erscheint in der Weise der in die Unverborgenheit sich* *bergenden Ankunft*]. [. . .] The difference of being and beings, as the differentiation of coming-over and arrival [*Unter-schied von Überkommnis und Ankunft*], is the accord [*Austrag*] of the two in *unconcealing keeping in concealment.*"[8] In fact, nothing is clearer than this phenomenological description of the *es gibt:* when it is given, or more precisely when *it gives* (understood in the trivial sense: when it functions, it works, it performs), the being arrives in visibility because it occupies and seizes visibility entirely (just as the arrival, *Ankunft,* of a train, precisely in the banal sense of the term, fills the station and focuses every gaze upon it). But beings can neither unleash nor prompt the visibility that they appropriate in this way: only being can open and uncover it, because it alone consists precisely in this display, because it alone comes from a coming-over *(Überkommnis),* opening the site that an arrival *(Ankunft)* will eventually occupy. This arrival receives its site, but by occupying it, it masks it and also renders invisible the coming-over that had opened it. By occupying the entire stage, beings make this very scene invisible. Being thus disappears in the visibility *(l'évidence)* of the being whose arrival covers up its nevertheless unconcealing coming-over. The being thus hides being from view by a phenomenological necessity which attests that being never shows itself *without* a being nor, moreover, *as* a being, as *Sein und Zeit* has already repeated with decisive insistence. The process of the givenness of the giving thus reproduces, here ontologically, in the agreement of being and the being according to the *es gibt,* the aporia of the gift in general, which Saint Augustine had described in a theological context.

It is characteristic of the gift given that it spontaneously conceals the givenness in it; thus a characteristic of the phenomenon of the gift is that it masks itself. Is it possible to locate the phenomenon of sacrifice within the essential aporia of the phenomenality of the gift? And, in being articulated there, might the phenomenon of sacrifice even allow us to solve the aporia of the gift?

IV. THE LIFTING OF THE GIVEN AND THE RELIEVING OF THE GIFT

By virtue of its visibility, the given constitutes an obstacle to that which makes this very visibility possible. What then makes the visibility of the gift possible, if not the process of givenness, whereby the giver turns the gift over as given, by handing it over in its autonomous visibility?

We should here note carefully that the gift given does not mask only (or even first of all) the giver, as an effect is detached from its efficient cause, or as the beneficiary of a favor refuses out of ingratitude to recognize it. The gift given masks the very process of giving givenness, a process in which the giver participates without constituting it intrinsically (he can even recuse himself without the process of giving being suspended). For, as we noted above, a gift (reduced) can remain perfectly possible and complete even with an anonymous or uncertain giver, or indeed without any confirmed giver. In fact, at issue here is one of the cardinal figures of the reduction of the gift to givenness. The question thus does not consist in reverting from the given to the giver, but in letting appear even in the gift ultimately given (in a being arrived in its arrival [*arrivage, Ankunft*] the advancing process of its coming-over, which delivers its visibility by giving it to the gift, or, more generally, the very coming-over that delivers the gift phenomenally (the *Überkommnis* that unconceals the visible). At issue would be the suspending of the gift given, so that it would allow the process of its givenness, namely, the given character of the gift (its given-ness [*donnéité*], to translate *Gegebenheit* literally), to appear in its own mode, instead of crushing it in the fall from the given into a pure and simple found object. So it is not a question of suppressing the gift given, for the benefit of the giver, but of making this gift transparent anew in its own process of givenness by letting its giver eventually appear there, and, first and always, by allowing to appear the coming-over that delivers the gift into the visible. At stake here is the phenomenality of this very return: to return to the gift given the phenomenality of its return, of the return that inscribes it through givenness in its visibility as gift coming from somewhere other than itself. The gift appears as such—in other words, as arriving from somewhere other than itself—only if it appears in such a way that it ceaselessly refers to this elsewhere that gives it, and from which it finds itself given to view.

That the gift given allows the return from which it proceeds to appear: this defines the signification and the phenomenological function of *sacrifice*—such is, at least, our hypothesis. To sacrifice does not signify to relinquish a good (by destruction or dispossession), even if this relinquishing were possibly for the other's benefit; rather, it consists in making appear the referral from which it proceeds, by reversing it (by making it return) toward the elsewhere, whose intrinsic, irrevocable, and permanent mark it bears insofar as it is a gift given.[9] Henceforth, sacrifice presupposes a gift already given, the point of which is neither destruction, its undoing, nor even its transfer to another owner, but, instead, its return to the givenness from which it proceeds, and whose mark it should always bear. Sacrifice gives the gift back to the givenness from which it proceeds, by returning it to the very return that originally constitutes it. Sacrifice does not separate itself from the gift but dwells in it totally. It manifests this by returning to the gift its givenness because it repeats the gift on the basis of its origin. The formula that perfectly captures the conditions of possibility of the gift is found in a verse from the Septuagint, ὅτι σὰ τὰ πάντα καὶ ἐκ τῶν σῶν δεδώκαμέν σοι—"all things are yours and it is by taking from among what is yours that we have given you gifts" (1 Chron. 29:14). To make a gift by taking from among gifts already given in order to re-give it; to "second" a gift from the first gift itself, to make a gift by reversing the first gift toward the one who gives it, and thus to make it appear through and through as a given arising from elsewhere—this is what accurately defines sacrifice, which consists in making visible the gift as given according to the coming-over of givenness. At issue is absolutely not a counter-gift, as if the giver needed either to recover his due (in the manner of an exchange), or to receive a supplementary tribute (gratitude as a symbolic compensation); rather, the point is the recognition of the gift as such, by repeating in reverse the process of givenness, and by reintegrating the gift to it, wresting it from its factual fall back to the rank (without givenness) of found object, non-given, *un-given*, in the end, to make visible not only the given but the process of givenness itself (as coming-over, *Überkommnis*), which would otherwise be left unnoticed, as if excluded from all phenomenality.

Sacrifice does not return the given to the giver by depriving the recipient *(donataire)* of the gift: it renders givenness visible by re-giving the gift. Sacrifice effects the redounding *(la redondance)* of the gift. As a result, sacrifice loses nothing, above all not the gift that it re-gives; on the contrary, it wins—it wins the gift, which it keeps all the more that it makes it appear for the first time as such, as a gift given, finally safeguarded in its givenness (given-ness, *Gegebenheit*). Sacrifice wins, but without even having to play the game of "loser wins" (as in the so-called pure love of God), as if it were necessary to lose much in order to win still more by retribution. Sacrifice wins by re-giving *(redondance):* it conquers the true phenomenon of the gift by restoring to it, through the act of re-giving, the phenomenality of givenness. Sacrifice re-gives the gift starting with the recipient and makes the gift appear as such in the light of its givenness and, sometimes, for the glory of the giver. In this, it corresponds to forgiveness *(le pardon):* forgiveness re-gives the gift as well, but starting from the giver, who confirms it in the light of givenness for the salvation of the recipient. Forgiveness and sacrifice correspond to one another in this way, so as to make the phenomenality of givenness appear by the double redounding of the gift, beginning either from the recipient, or from the giver.

V. THE CONFIRMATION OF ABRAHAM

Thus we have determined sacrifice according to its phenomenality by inscribing it within the framework of a phenomenology of the gift: its function is to make appear what the gift, once given, never fails to cover over and hide—the process of givenness itself—such that on the basis of a review of this process, the giver eventually becomes visible again as well. Can we confirm this determination of sacrifice by a significant example? Certainly, if we consider the episode of the sacrifice of Abraham, or rather of the sacrifice of Isaac by Abraham, related in Genesis 22:1–19. Without glossing over its radically theological status (indeed, how could one do so?), we shall sketch an interpretation of it first according to the principle of the phenomenality of sacrifice.

Certainly, there is a sacrifice involved, specified as such: "[O]ffer [your son Isaac . . .] as a burnt offering upon one of the mountains of which I shall tell you" (22:2)—but it is a sacrifice that precisely does *not* take place, at least if one confines oneself to the common determination of sacrifice (a destruction or dispossession allowing an exchange within the framework of a contract). Understanding this sacrifice presupposes, paradoxically, understanding why Isaac has *not* been sacrificed ("Abraham went and took the ram, and offered it up as a burnt offering instead of his son," 22:13). Or more precisely, it involves understanding why, while there was no sacrifice following the common understanding (no destruction of Isaac), there was indeed, according to the biblical account, fulfilment of the obligation toward God, since God acknowledges: "[N]ow I know that you fear God" (22:12). Now this is possible only if we grant that this account does not follow the common determination of sacrifice, but instead follows its phenomenological concept—that of sacrifice conceived on the basis of the gift, and of the gift reduced to givenness. It is here that we must therefore locate the concept. A first moment seems evident: God demands of Abraham a sacrifice, and even a consuming sacrifice (where the victim is consumed in fire, leaving nothing to share between God, the priest, and the one offering, in contrast to other forms of sacrifices). This demand of sacrifice falls upon Isaac, the one and only son of Abraham. Do we have here a sacrifice according to the common concept? Precisely not, because God asks nothing out of the ordinary of Abraham, nor does he enter into any contractual agreement with him; he simply and justifiably takes back Isaac, who already belongs to him, and even doubly so. First, quite obviously, because all first-borns belong to God by right: "The first-born of your sons you shall give to me. You shall do likewise with your oxen and with your sheep; seven days it shall be with its dam; on the eighth day you shall give it to me" (Exod. 22:29–30). Or again: "Consecrate to me all the first-born; whatever is the first to open the womb among the people of Israel, both of man and of beast, is mine" (Exod. 13:2). The question consists only in knowing what this belonging and this consecration really imply. The answer varies, from actual putting to death (in the case of the plague on the firstborn of Egypt, Exod. 12:29–30), to the ritual sacrifice of animals in the Temple, right up to the redemption of the firstborn of Israel, prescribed explicitly by God (Exod. 13:11–15, 34:19; Num. 18:14), who forbids human sacrifices.[10] In this sense, Isaac belongs first to God, before belonging to his father (Abraham), in the same way as any other firstborn, of Israel or of any other people.

God has nevertheless another right of possession over Isaac, radical in another way: Isaac in effect does *not* belong to Abraham, who could not, neither he, nor his wife, on their own, engender him ("Now Abraham and Sarah were old, advanced in age; and it had ceased to be with Sarah after the manner of women," Gen. 18:11). Thus, Isaac belongs from the beginning and as a miracle to God alone: "Nothing, neither word nor deed, remains impossible for God. At the same season next year, I will return to your home and Sarah will have a son."[11] And in fact, "The Lord visited Sarah as he had said, and the Lord did to Sarah as he had promised. And Sarah conceived, and bore Abraham a son in his old age at the time of which God had spoken to him" (21:1–2). Thus, by right, Isaac, child of the promise through divine omnipotence, comes to Abraham only as a pure gift, unexpected because beyond every hope, incommensurate with what Abraham would have possessed or engendered himself. But this gift nevertheless disappears as soon as Isaac appears as such, that is to say, as the son of Abraham, or more precisely, as the one whom Abraham claims as his son: "Abraham called the name of his son who was

THE REASON OF THE GIFT

born to him, whom Sarah bore to him, Isaac. [. . .] And the child grew, and was weaned; and Abraham made a great feast on the day that Isaac was weaned" (21:3, 8). And for her part, Sarah, too, appropriates Isaac as *her* son ("I have borne him a son in his old age!" 21:7), since she drives out as a competitor the other son, natural born, whom Abraham had had with Hagar (21:9–14). And the call that God addresses to Abraham aims only to denounce explicitly this improper appropriation: "Take your son, your only son Isaac, whom you cherish"—because Isaac precisely *is not* the possession of Abraham, who therefore must not cherish him as such. The demand for a sacrifice opposes to this illegitimate appropriation, which cancels the gift given in a possession, the most original right of the giver to have his gift acknowledged as a gift given, which is to say, simply acknowledged as an always provisional, transferable, and alienable usufruct: "Go to the land of Moriah, and offer him there as a burnt offering" (22:2). Abraham hears himself asked not so much to kill his son, to lose him and return possession of him to God (according to the common concept of the gift), as, first and foremost, to give back to him his status as gift, precisely to return him to his status as gift given by reducing him (leading him back) to givenness.

And Abraham accomplishes this reduction in the most explicit and clear manner imaginable. Isaac, who reasons according to the common concept of the gift, of course notices that his father does not have (that is to say, does not *possess*) any possession available to sacrifice (to destroy and to exchange in the framework of a contract): "[W]here is the lamb for a burnt offering?" (22:7). Abraham, who already reasons according to the phenomenological concept of sacrifice, as gift given reduced to givenness, answers that "God will provide himself the lamb for a burnt offering" (22:8)—which means that God decides everything, including what one will offer him, and thus that neither Abraham, nor even Isaac, will be able to give anything to God, except what God, himself and in the first place, has already given to them; in a word, this means that every gift made to God comes first from God as a gift given to us. The place of sacrifice is thus called "God provides" (22:14). It should be pointed out here that the Hebrew says יִרְאֶה *yir'eh* (from the root ראה *r'h*, to see, to foresee, to provide), but that the Septuagint first understands, for the name Abraham attaches to the mountain, *God saw*, εἶδεν (second aorist of ὁράω), and then, for the name that it later retains, ὤφθη, *God appears* (passive aorist of ὁράω). Thus, it is as if the fact that God sees and provides, and therefore quite clearly *gives* the offering of the sacrifice, or put another way, *gives the gift to give*, that is, makes the gift appear as such, given by the giver—were equivalent to the appearing of the giver, to the fact that God *gives himself to seeing*. So God gives himself to be seen as he gives originally, as he shows that every gift comes from him. He appears as the giver that the gifts manifest by referring to him as their origin and provenance.

Abraham, and he alone (not Isaac), sees in this way that God alone gives the gift of the burnt offering, such that God subsequently appears to him. But he had already recognized God as the giver of gifts from the moment that he had finally agreed to recognize Isaac as for him the principal among the gifts given by God, and thus due to God. So it is no longer important that Abraham kill, eliminate, and exchange his son for God's benefit in order to accomplish the sacrifice demanded (according to the common concept of sacrifice); rather, it matters exclusively (according to the phenomenological concept of the gift) that he acknowledge his son as a gift, that he accomplish this recognition of the gift by giving it back to its giver, and, thus, that he let God appear through his gift, rightly recognized *as a gift given*. God clearly understands it as such since he spares Isaac. It is important to note that to the extent that he restrains Abraham from killing Isaac, God specifically *does not* refuse his sacrifice, but nullifies only the putting to death, because the putting to death does not belong to the essence of sacrifice: the actual death of Isaac would have ratified only sacrifice in its common concept (destruction, dispossession, exchange, and contract). In fact, God lets Abraham go right to the end of sacrifice, but understood in the sense of its phenomenological concept: the recognition of

Isaac as a gift received from God and due to God. And in order to recognize it, one need only acknowledge Abraham's loss of Isaac, a recognition accomplished perfectly without his being put to death, and from the moment he is accepted as a boundless gift: "The angel said, 'Do not lay your hand on the lad or do anything to him; for now I know that you fear God, seeing you have not withheld your son, your only son, from me'" (22:12). By refusing to let Isaac be put to death, God does not thereby refuse to acknowledge the gift offered by Abraham; he accepts the sacrifice all the more, understood this time in the strict phenomenological sense. By sparing Isaac, henceforth recognized (by Abraham) as a gift (from God), God re-gives Isaac to him, gives him a second time, presenting a gift by a redounding *(don par une redondance)*, which consecrates it definitively as a gift henceforth held in common and, ultimately, transparently between the giver and the recipient. The sacrifice redoubles the gift and confirms it as such for the first time.[12]

VI. SACRIFICE IN TRUTH

Thus sacrifice requires neither destruction, nor restitution, nor even exchange, much less a contract, because its basis is not the economy (which dispenses with the gift), but the gift itself, whose aporia it endeavors to work through. For the function of sacrifice is only to allow the recognition of the giver and, through him, the entire process of givenness, by reducing the given. In *this* sense, sacrifice can be understood as a destruction, but a destruction taken in the sense of *Abbau*, of the deconstruction that frees by putting into the light of day what accumulation had covered up. Sacrifice destroys the given, by clearing it away in order to uncover that which had made it visible and possible—the advance of givenness itself. This deconstructive and uncovering destruction can thus be better named a reduction: the bracketing of the gift given allows the giver's gesture to rise again to the visible, makes the recipient recover the posture of reception, and above all gives movement back to the coming-over of givenness in each of the three terms involved (giver, recipient, and gift given). Sacrifice is a redounding of the gift originating with the recipient (just as forgiveness [*le pardon*] consists of the redounding of the gift from the giver). In this way one succeeds in raising the epistemological obstacle of an economic conception of sacrifice by recognizing that "to sacrifice is not to kill, but to abandon and to give" (Bataille),[13] to the point that it becomes possible to conceive, as Levinas puts it, an "approach of the Infinite through sacrifice."[14] It constitutes an approach to the infinite because the reduction of the ever-finite given opens the only royal way toward the illumination of a possible infinite—not a being, even one that is given, and even less a necessarily determined and possessable object, but the process of an arrival *(une advenue)*, always come from elsewhere and, for that very reason, inalienable and unavailable. Unless the very access to being depends on sacrifice, if, like Patočka (and doubtless in opposition to Heidegger), one decides to think the *es gibt* resolutely, on the basis of givenness, such that givenness requires sacrifice, but also alone renders sacrifice intelligible: "In sacrifice, *es gibt* being: here Being already 'gives' itself to us, not in a refusal but explicitly. To be sure, only a man capable of experiencing, in something so apparently negative, the coming of Being, only as he begins to sense that this lack opens access to what is richest, to that which bestows everything and presents all as gift to all, only then can he begin to experience this favor."[15] Which can finally be transposed into theological terms, for it may be that Saint Augustine says nothing different when he defines sacrifices as "opera [. . .] misericordiae, sive in nos ipsos, sive in proximos, quae *referuntur ad Deum* [works of mercy shown to ourselves or to our neighbours, and done with reference to God]."[16]

Notes

Introduction

1. "Analytic Kantianism" encompasses a fairly large group of philosophers; here I will only be considering aspects of the thought of Wilfrid Sellars and John McDowell, leaving out any discussion of such figures as P. F. Strawson or Robert Brandom. For a more comprehensive view of "analytic Kantianism," see the articles collected and edited by James Conant in the special issue of *Philosophical Topics* devoted to "analytic Kantianism": *Philosophical Topics* 34, nos. 1 and 2 (Spring and Fall 2006). McDowell's contribution to this volume, "Sensory Consciousness in Kant and Sellars," is included in his *Having the World in View: Essays on Kant, Hegel, and Sellars* (Cambridge, MA: Harvard University Press, 2009), 108–26. For a good brief summary of some of the important issues involved in both McDowell's and Brandom's respective engagements with Sellars, Kantianism, and Hegelian thought, see Paul Redding, "The Possibility of German Idealism after Analytic Philosophy: McDowell, Brandom and Beyond," in *Postanalytic and Metacontinental: Crossing Philosophical Divides*, ed. Jack Reynolds et al. (New York: Continuum, 2010), 191–202, especially the section entitled "Paths from Pittsburgh to Berlin."

2. Jean-Luc Marion, *Réduction et donation: Recherches sur Husserl, Heidegger et la phénoménologie* (Paris: Presses Universitaires de France, 1989); *Reduction and Givenness: Investigations of Husserl, Heidegger, and Phenomenology*, trans. Thomas A. Carlson (Evanston, IL: Northwestern University Press, 1998). Subsequent citations will be indicated by the abbreviations *RD/RG*, followed by the page numbers. Likewise for Jean-Luc Marion, *Étant donné: Essai d'une phénoménologie de la donation* (Paris: Presses Universitaires de France, 1997, 2nd ed. 1998); *Being Given: Toward a Phenomenology of Givenness*, trans. Jeffrey L. Kosky (Stanford, CA: Stanford University Press,

2002). Citations will be given in the text, with page numbers following the abbreviations *ED/BG*.

3. Kevin Hart, introduction to *Counter-Experiences: Reading Jean-Luc Marion*, ed. Hart (Notre Dame, IN: University of Notre Dame Press, 2007), 13.

4. Ibid.

5. Antonio López, review of Jean-Luc Marion's *Being Given: Toward a Phenomenology of Givenness*, in *Review of Metaphysics* 57, no. 4 (June 2004): 855, referring to *ED* §26, 360–73/*BG* 261–71.

6. Jean-Luc Marion, *Certitudes négatives* (Paris: Fayard, 2010), 299. Subsequent citations of this book will be given parenthetically, following the abbreviation *CN*. Translations are my own.

7. On birth, see Jean-Luc Marion, *De surcroît: Études sur les phénomènes saturés* (Paris: Presses Universitaires de France, 2001), 49–52; *In Excess: Studies of Saturated Phenomena*, trans. Robyn Horner and Vincent Berraud (New York: Fordham University Press, 2002), 41–44. See also *CN* 291–99. Marion's account of birth is heavily indebted, as Marion himself acknowledges, to the analyses of Claude Romano in *L'événement et le monde* (Paris: Presses Universitaires de France, 1998), 95–101; *Event and World*, trans. Shane Mackinlay (New York: Fordham University Press, 2009), 69–73. However, Shane Mackinlay draws distinctions between Marion's approach to birth, which Mackinlay characterizes as "narrow[ly]" focused upon the *ego*, and Romano's, which Mackinlay finds focused upon the "interrelatedness" of the I who is born and the world into which he or she is born in the event of being born. See Shane Mackinlay, *Interpreting Excess: Jean-Luc Marion, Saturated Phenomena, and Hermeneutics* (New York: Fordham University Press, 2010), 50. Subsequent citations from Mackinlay's book will be given parenthetically.

8. For a striking description of the experience of givenness as, fundamentally, an experience of *dependence* best illustrated by the phenomenon of birth, see Luigi Giussani, *Il senso religioso* (Milano: Rizzoli, 1997), 139, 141; *The Religious Sense*, trans. John Zucchi (Montreal and Kingston: McGill-Queen's University Press, 1997), 100, 101: "Supponete di nascere, di uscire dal ventre di vostra madre all'età che avete in questo momento, nel senso di sviluppo e di coscienza così come vi è possibile averli adesso. Quale sarebbe il primo, l'assolutamente primo sentimento, cioè il primo fattore della reazione di fronte al reale? [. . .] Io apro gli occhi a questa realtà che mi si impone, che non dipende da me, ma da cui io dipendo: il grande condizionamento della mia esistenza, se volete, il dato." (Picture yourself being born, coming out of your mother's womb at the age you are now at this very moment in terms of your development and consciousness. What would be the first, absolutely your initial reaction? [. . .] I open my eyes to this reality which imposes itself upon me, which does not depend upon me, but upon

which I depend; it is the great conditioning of my existence—if you like, the given.)

9. Jean-Luc Marion, "The Banality of Saturation," trans. Jeffrey L. Kosky, in *Counter-Experiences: Reading Jean-Luc Marion*, ed. Kevin Hart (Notre Dame, IN: University of Notre Dame Press, 2007), 383–418, on 408; "La banalité de la saturation," in *Le visible et le révélé* (Paris: Cerf, 2005), 180.

10. Marion, "The Banality of Saturation," 408, trans. modified; "La banalité de la saturation," 180.

11. "Counter-experience" was first discussed by Marion in *Étant donné*, §22, 300–302; *Being Given*, 215–16. He then describes it in more detail in "The Banality of Saturation," 401–4, and, most recently, at various places in *Certitudes négatives*—see, e.g., 317.

12. Wilfrid Sellars, "Empiricism and the Philosophy of Mind," in *Science, Perception and Reality* (London: Routledge and Kegan Paul, 1963), 127–96. Originally published in *The Foundations of Science and the Concepts of Psychology and Psychoanalysis*, ed. Herbert Feigl and Michael Scriven, Minnesota Studies in the Philosophy of Science, vol. 1 (Minneapolis: University of Minnesota Press, 1956). The 1963 edition will hereafter be cited parenthetically, using the abbreviation EPM. McDowell's *Mind and World* (Cambridge, MA: Harvard University Press, 1994, 1996) will be cited parenthetically using the abbreviation *MW*.

13. Calls for a confrontation between respective approaches to the given in Sellars and in Marion have been made by Jean Grondin, "La tension de la donation ultime et de la pensée herméneutique de l'application chez Jean-Luc Marion," *Dialogue* 38 (1999): 547–59, on 552; and Denis Fisette, "Phénoménologie et métaphysique: Remarques à propos d'un débat récent," in *La métaphysique: Son histoire, sa critique, ses enjeux*, ed. Jean-Marc Narbonne and Luc Langlois (Paris: Vrin/Laval: Les Presses de l'Université Laval, 1999), 91–116, in 111n1. In his recent study of *Gegebenheit* in relation to the motifs of reduction, construction, and destruction in Heidegger, Husserl, and Natorp, Jean-François Courtine similarly suggests—but does not pursue—the usefulness of "confronting [this dossier] with other, later debates relative to the given or the 'myth of the given.'" See Jean-François Courtine, "Réduction, construction, destruction. D'un dialogue à trois: Natorp, Husserl, Heidegger," *Philosophiques* 36, no. 2 (Automne 2009): 559–77, on 560. Hent de Vries, in his ninety-eight-page introductory essay to the volume *Religion: Beyond a Concept* (New York: Fordham University Press, 2008), discusses Sellars, Richard Rorty, and Robert Brandom, including the role of the "myth of the given" in this line of thought, suggesting along the way (alas, with nothing in the way of supporting arguments) that aspects of Marion's thought are compatible with the pragmatic perspectivalism of these three American philosophers (see 53, 64).

14. Claude Romano, *Au coeur de la raison, la phénoménologie* (Paris: Gallimard/Folio Essais, 2010). Citations will be provided parenthetically. Translations from this book are my own.

15. Martin Heidegger, *Grundprobleme der Phänomenologie* (1919/20), *Anhang A*, ed. Hans-Helmuth Gander, in *GA* 58 (Frankfurt a./M.: Vittorio Klostermann, 1993), 131; quoted by Marion, 36.

16. Marion points out that Heidegger distinguishes "two primary meanings of givenness" in the neo-Kantian field: "on one side that of Natorp, who only allows 'a givenness [*Gegebenheit*] that derives in a precise sense from the accomplishment of science,' and thus remains within it without exempting itself from it; on the other that of Rickert, who allows 'a givenness [*Gegebenheit*] that is *anteriorly-given* [*vorgegeben*], by necessity of meaning, to this accomplishment [of science] and its possible use.' Thus we understand [. . .] in what way givenness was marking out a crossroads in philosophy [. . .], where two accepted meanings of *Erkenntnistheorie* diverge, according to whether the given is inscribed within the knowledge of the object [Rickert] or precedes and determines it irreducibly [Natorp]" 40–41.

17. Romano writes, "The confrontation of phenomenology with the thought of Sellars and of McDowell, respectively, is in no way a mere stylistic exercise. The problem of what, across the Atlantic, has come to be called 'the non-conceptual content' of experience has seen a lively growth in interest during the last two decades, under the impulse of Evans, McDowell, Peacocke and others. This problem is the very same one that occupied Husserl when he enlarged experiential sense beyond conceptual sense. But the confrontation of these two traditions cannot have real philosophical significance unless we are capable of showing first that they possess a common background: that of neo-Kantianism" (734).

18. Michael Friedman, in his historically based critique of McDowell's *Mind and World* entitled "Exorcising the Philosophical Tradition" (in *Reading McDowell: On Mind and World*, ed. Nicholas H. Smith [London: Routledge, 2002], 25–57), makes some points similar to those made by Romano (738–39) about the structuring role of language in the "logical idealism" of the Marburg school of neo-Kantianism (Hermann Cohen, Paul Natorp, and Ernst Cassirer), and the similarity between that way of arguing for the thoroughly conceptual nature of experience and McDowell's Gadamer-influenced view that "languages and traditions can figure [. . .] as constitutive of our unproblematic openness to the world" (*MW* 155) (see Friedman, 39, on the Marburg school, and 46–48 on language as harmonizing mind and world in *Mind and World*). McDowell himself responds to all the essays in this volume; unfortunately he does not engage with this critical observation of a continuity between his thought and that of the Marburg school, other than to "express an affinity [. . .] with Kant's successors" (see Smith, *Reading McDowell*, 274).

19. An exploration of the persuasiveness of Romano's arguments for these conclusions is beyond the scope of this introduction; see Romano, 756–60, for his conclusions about several of Sellars's arguments in EPM, and 760–78 for those having to do with the central aspects of McDowell's argument in *Mind and World*. For a nonhistorical comparison of the given in Sellars and Husserl that agrees at several points with Romano's conclusions, but also explores divergences between Husserl and Sellars surrounding the issues of intentionality and intersubjectivity, see Gail Soffer, "Revisiting the Myth: Husserl and Sellars on the Given," *Review of Metaphysics* 57, no. 2 (December 2003): 301–37.

20. "To McDowell's eyes, the content of experience is conceptual to be sure, in the sense of propositional—we perceive *that things are thus and so—* but, even when experience possesses the same 'content' as the judgment made upon it, it is not intrinsically a judgment. We are thus watching the third act in the debate between empiricism and neo-Kantianism—a neo-Kantianism whose weaker and weaker claims nonetheless remain inside the magic circle of formulations and of problems out of which it is unable to extract itself. After the original neo-Kantianism's debate with classical empiricism, after that of Sellars with logical empiricism, McDowell attacks a residue of givenness that might still tempt the philosopher, in spite of Sellars's critiques, and which would make felt the heavy threat of a new cleavage between sensibility and understanding, or, as he likes to say in appealing to Kant, between receptivity and spontaneity" (Romano, 760–61).

21. Marlène Zarader, "Phenomenality and Transcendence," in *Transcendence in Philosophy and Religion*, ed. James E. Faulconer (Bloomington: Indiana University Press, 2003), 106–19, quotations from 114 and 116; for Marion's response to Zarader, see "La banalité de la saturation," especially 148–49; trans. Kosky, 386–88.

22. *MW* 23. What is "intolerable" is the anxiety-filled oscillation between coherentism and the Myth of the Given (*MW* 15).

23. Zarader characterizes her elimination of pure transcendence as an act of "subversion": "Subversion [differs from destruction in that it] acknowledges its own impurity and interminability: it knows it can never extract itself from the place that it contests; nevertheless, it strives continuously to upset and to divert that place" (117). Zarader credits Roland Barthes as the source of this concept of subversion; it is also characteristic of the guilty complicity that characterizes Georges Bataille's practice of contestation.

24. Romano, 755–56, points out that among the many possible senses of "looks," Sellars privileges the comparative.

25. Anthony J. Steinbock, "The Poor Phenomenon: Marion and the Problem of Givenness," in *Words of Life: New Theological Turns in French Phenomenology*, ed. Bruce Ellis Benson and Norman Wirzba (New York: Fordham University Press, 2010), 120–31, quotation from 129.

26. Steinbock, "The Poor Phenomenon," 129.

27. In *Le phénomène érotique: Six méditations* (Paris: Grasset, 2003), 140; *The Erotic Phenomenon*, trans. Stephen E. Lewis (Chicago: University of Chicago Press, 2007), 87, Marion writes that "the properly infinite excess of the lover, as he loves without condition of reciprocity," is characterized by "unknowing" and "poverty." It seems, then, that the erotic phenomenon revises significantly even the "essential finitude" of the gifted that Steinbock, following what is written in *Being Given*, references in his discussion of the decision for or against the saturated phenomenon (see previous note). For more on the infinity of the lover's advance, see my essay "The Lover's Capacity in Jean-Luc Marion's *The Erotic Phenomenon*," *Quaestiones Disputatae* 1, no. 1 (Fall 2010): 226–44, especially 239–42.

1. The Phenomenological Origins of the Concept of Givenness

1. I first introduced this quasi principle as a conclusion to Jean-Luc Marion, *Réduction et donation: Études sur Husserl, Heidegger et la phénoménologie* (Paris: Presses Universitaires de France, 1989, 2004), 303; *Reduction and Givenness: Investigations of Husserl, Heidegger, and Phenomenology*, trans. Thomas A. Carlson (Evanston, IL: Northwestern University Press, 1998), 203. After Michel Henry had validated it in its essential thesis in "Les quatres principes de la phénoménologie," *Revue de Métaphysique et de Morale* 1 (1991), reprinted in Henry, *Phénoménologie de la vie*, t. 1: *De la phénoménologie* (Paris: Presses Universitaires de France, 2003), I developed it in Marion, *Étant donné: Essai d'une phénoménologie de la donation* (Paris: Presses Universitaires de France, 1997, 2005), §§1–6; *Being Given: Toward a Phenomenology of Givenness*, trans. Jeffrey L. Kosky (Stanford, CA: Stanford University Press, 2002), §§1–6.

2. To render *Gegebenheit* as given-ness (*donnéité*), rather than as given (*donné*) or givenness (*donation*), has been suggested by several translators of Husserl (for the different possible translations, see *Étant donné*, 98), especially Jean-François Lavigne, *Husserl et la naissance de la phénoménologie (1900–1913)* (Paris: Presses Universitaires de France, 2005), 175.

3. This was Dominique Janicaud's crucial point in his *Le tournant théologique de la phénoménologie française* (Combas: L'Eclat, 1991); Dominique Janicaud, et al., *Phenomenology and the "Theological Turn": The French Debate* (New York: Fordham University Press, 2000).

4. Jean-Luc Marion, "L'autre philosophie première et la question de la donation," *Philosophie* 49 (Paris, 1996), included in Marion, *De surcroît: Études sur les phénomènes saturés* (Paris: Presses Universitaires de France, 2001); *In Excess: Studies of Saturated Phenomena*, trans. Robyn Horner and Vincent Berraud (New York: Fordham University Press, 2002), chap. 1; and then in *Étant donné*, book 1.

5. I attempted to show this in *Étant donné*, §3, 53 ff.; *Being Given*, 34 ff.

6. Published by Bernd Heimbüchel, under the title *Zur Bestimmung der Philosophie*, in *Gesamtausgabe*, Bd. 56/57 (Frankfurt a./M.: Vittorio Klostermann, 1987). I have attempted a brief commentary in "Ce que donne 'Cela donne,'" in *Le souci du passage: Mélanges offerts à Jean Greisch*, ed. Philippe Capelle, Geneviève Hébert, and Marie-Dominique Popelard (Paris: Cerf, 2004), 293–306.

7. Martin Heidegger, *Sein und Zeit*, 10th ed. (Tübingen: Max Niemeyer, 1996), principally the *Gegebenheit des Ich* (§25, 115 and 116); of the totality of *Dasein* (§41, 191; §62, 309); and of *Erlebnisse* (§53, 265). I adopt as my own Jean-François Courtine's remark: "[. . .] the Heideggerian 'es gibt,' as it appears well before the last variations of *Zeit und Sein* in *Sein und Zeit*, [. . .] indicate[s], moreover within quotation marks, that interpretation is necessary, that Being *is not*, but that it gives Being [*il y a Être*]" (Courtine, introduction to Alexius Meinong, *Théorie de l'objet et Présentation personnelle*, trans. into French by Courtine and M. de Launay [Paris: J. Vrin, 1999], 34). In a sense, my essay here is merely an attempt to interpret these quotation marks.

8. Martin Heidegger, *Sein und Zeit*, §2, 6–7; *Being and Time*, trans. Joan Stambaugh (Albany: State University of New York Press, 1996), 5 (trans. modified). In his personal copy, Heidegger notes that *Dasein* here remains "neither the usual concept nor any other."

9. I adopt as my own Courtine's apt remark on the ". . . 'es gibt,' which both the French 'il y a' and the English 'there is' translate badly. Indeed, with 'es gibt' we are in front of a figure that is clearly elementary, extenuated as much as one might wish, and reduced to an almost nothing (but nevertheless not nothing) of givenness or of given being" (introduction to Meinong, *Théorie de l'objet*, 34; see my *Étant donné*, 51; *Being Given*, 33). But why speak from the outset of an *extenuation*? On the contrary, it may be that *es gibt* supports no analogy or gradation at all, but instead either produces itself perfectly, or does not produce itself at all, precisely because it indicates a fact, or indeed an event. What is more, can one legitimately make an equivalence between givenness and given *being*, if the whole point is precisely to think that ". . . Being *is not*"? This isn't simply about a detail; or rather, everything here is at stake in such details.

10. For example, *Sein und Zeit*, §7, 36; §12, 55; §18, 87; §33, 158; §49, 247; §52, 258; §72, 30.

11. *Sein und Zeit*, §16, 72; trans. Stambaugh, 67–68 (trans. modified). Couldn't one bring together the distinction between two modes of innerworldy beings: "Aber Zuhandenes 'gibt es' doch nur auf dem Grunde von Vorhandenem" (§15, 71)?

12. *Sein und Zeit*, §44, 230; trans. Stambaugh, 211 (trans. modified).

13. *Sein und Zeit*, §41, 196; trans. Stambaugh, 183 (see also §43, 207 and 208).

14. *Sein und Zeit*, §4: "Es ist vielmehr dadurch ontisch ausgezeichnet, daß es diesem Seienden in seinem Sein *um* dieses Sein selbst geht" (12); "Rather it is ontically distinguished by the fact that in its being this being is concerned *about* its very being" (trans. Stambaugh, 10).

15. *Sein und Zeit*, §43, 212; trans. Stambaugh, 196 (trans. modified).

16. *Sein und Zeit*, §44, 226; trans. Stambaugh, 208 (trans. modified). Similarly, *"Warum müssen wir voraussetzen, daß es Wahrheit gibt?* Was heißt 'voraussetzen'? Was meint das 'müssen' und 'wir'? Was besagt: 'Es gibt Wahrheit'?" (227; trans. Stambaugh, 209, modified: *"Why must we presuppose that it gives truth?* What does 'presuppose' mean? What do 'must' and 'we' mean? What does it mean 'it gives truth'?").

17. *Sein und Zeit*, §80, 411; trans. Stambaugh, 378 (trans. modified).

18. *Sein und Zeit*, §79, 411; trans. Stambaugh, 377 (trans. modified).

19. *Sein und Zeit*, §16, 72; trans. Stambaugh, 67–68 (modified) (cited in n. 11 above).

20. Emil Lask, *Zum System der Philosophie*, chap. 1, in *Gesammelte Schriften*, ed. Eugen Herrigel (Tübingen: Verlag von J. C. B. Mohr [Paul Siebeck], 1924), vol. 3, 179–80. The text takes up and refounds *Die Logik der Philosophie und die Kategorienlehre*, which Heidegger read from its publication in 1911. The major thesis there was already givenness: "Durch die Identität ist das bloße Etwas ein Gegenstand, ein Etwas, das 'es gibt.' Die Kategorie des 'Es-Gebens' ist die reflexive Gegenständlichkeit" (*Gesammelte Schriften*, vol. 2, 142). On this point, see the classic article by Theodore Kisiel, "Why Students of Heidegger Will Have to Read Emil Lask," *Man and World* 28 (1995), included in Kisiel, *Heidegger's Way of Thought: Critical and Interpretive Signposts* (New York: Continuum, 2002), 101–36.

21. *Sein und Zeit*, §2, 6–7 (cited in n. 8, above).

22. Heinrich Rickert, *Der Gegenstand der Erkenntnis: Einführung in die Transzendental-Philosophie* (Tübingen: J. C. B. Mohr, 1892, 5th ed. 1921), 326. (Heidegger cites the third edition, 1915, in *GA* 56/57, p. 34, and in *GA* 58, pp. 71, 226, in order to critique the confusion between two meanings of *Gegebenheit*: that which precedes the accomplishment of scientific knowledge, and that which proceeds from it).

23. Rickert, *Der Gegenstand der Erkenntnis*, 327, 328.

24. Paul Natorp, *Allgemeine Psychologie nach kritischer Methode. Erstes Buch: Objekt und Methode der Psychologie* (Tübingen: Verlag von J. C. B. Mohr [Paul Siebeck], 1912), chap. 3, §1, 40.

25. See Christoph von Wolzogen, "'Es gibt': Heidegger und Natorps 'Praktische Philosophie,'" in *Heidegger und die praktische Philosophie*, ed. Annemarie Gethmann-Seifert and Otto Pöggeler (Frankfurt a./M.: Suhrkamp, 1988).

26. Edmund Husserl, *Die Idee der Phänomenologie*, in *Gesammelte Werke*, Hua. 2 (The Hague: Martinus Nijhoff, 1950), 74; *The Idea of Phenomenol-*

ogy, trans. William P. Alston and George Nakhnikian (Dordrecht: Kluwer Academic Publishers, 1990), 59 (trans. modified).

27. *Die Idee der Phänomenologie*, 61; trans. Alston and Nakhnikian, 49 (trans. modified).

28. *Die Idee der Phänomenologie*, 44; trans. Alston and Nahknikian, 34 (trans. modified). On this strict link between *Gegebenheit* and reduction, see *Étant donné*, §3, 42 ff.; *Being Given*, §3, 27 ff.

29. *Die Idee der Phänomenologie*, 74; trans. Alston and Nahknikian, 59 (trans. modified).

30. *Die Idee der Phänomenologie*, 74; trans. Alston and Nahknikian, 59 (trans. modified). After 1907 Husserl will discover other "modes of authentic givenness," in particular, the flesh, passive syntheses, intersubjectivity, and teleology. Subsequent phenomenology will not stop adding more (being/beings, time, world and truth, the face, auto-affection, hermeneutics and differance, etc.). I hold that all come under givenness, whether one admits it or not.

31. Bernard Bolzano, *Wissenschaftslehre*, §67, in *Gesamtausgabe*, ed. Edmund Winter and J. Berg, Reihe 1: *Schriften*, Bd. 2, T. 2 (Stuttgart–Bad Cannstatt: Frommann, 1987), 112; *Theory of Science*, ed. Jan Berg, trans. Burnham Terrell (Dordrecht and Boston: D. Reidel, 1973), 106 (trans. modified).

32. Jocelyn Benoist, *Représentations sans objets: Aux origines de la phénoménologie et de la philosophie analytique* (Paris: Presses Universitaires de France, 2001), 19, an imprecise formulation in a work that is otherwise indispensable.

33. Who was nevertheless an essential relay for the question for Husserl. The dossier of their exchanges has been remarkably collected by Jacques English: Husserl-Twardowski, *Sur les objets intentionnels, 1893–1901* (Paris: Vrin, 1993).

34. Alexius Meinong, *Über Gegenstandstheorie* (originally published as *Untersuchungen zur Gegenstandstheorie und Psychologie* [Leipzig: Johann Ambrosius Barth, 1904]), §3, in *Gesamtausgabe*, ed. Rudolf Haller, Bd. 2. *Abhandlungen zur Erkenntnistheorie und Gegenstandstheorie* (Graz: Akademische Druck- u. Verlagsanstalt, 1971), 490. In a desire to remain elegant, the French translation ("Il y a des objets à propos desquels on peut affirmer qu'il n'y en a pas") misses the essential, *Gegebenheit*. Moreover, it hides or mars by elsewhere rendering it "être-donné" (§6), precisely there where givenness dispenses with being. See Alexius Meinong, *Théorie de l'objet et Présentation personelle*, with an instructive introduction by Jean-François Courtine (here, 73 and 83).

35. *Über Gegenstandstheorie*, §6, 500: "Unter Voraussetzung einer unbegrenzt leistungsfähigen Intelligenz also gibt es nichts Unerkennbares, und was erkennbar ist, das gibt es auch, oder, weil 'es gibt doch vorzugsweise von Seiendem, ja speziell von Existierendem gesagt zu werden pflegt, wäre es

vielleicht deutlicher, zu sagen: Alles Erkennbare ist gegeben—dem Erkennen nämlich. Und sofern alle Gegenstände erkennbar sind, kann ihnen ohne Ausnahme, mögen sie sein oder nicht sein, Gegebenheit als eine Art allgemeinster Eigenschaft nachgesagt werden" (where clearly one must not translate *Gegebenheit* by *being-given;* see the French translation by Courtine and de Launay, 83). See "die Gegenstandstheorie beschäftige sich mit dem Gegebenen ganz ohne Rücksicht auf dessen Sein" (§11, 519).

36. *Über Gegenstandstheorie,* §4, 494. See: "Der Gegenstand ist von Natur *außerseiend,* obwohl von seinen beiden Seinsobjektiven, seinem Sein und seinem Nichtsein, jedenfalls eines besteht." Which thus becomes the "principle of the beyond of being of the pure object, *Satz vom Außersein des reinen Gegenstandes,*" and certainly supposes the Kantian assumption that "being and non-being are equally exterior to the object," because they do not constitute real predicates (ibid.).

37. *Über Gegenstandstheorie,* §11, 521.

38. How can Benoist put into question the central role of givenness as such for Meinong ("It is nevertheless doubtful that this *reference* to modes of thought and to what *seems* to be the imperative of givenness are really so central in Meinongian analysis" (*Représentations sans objets,* 123, my emphasis)? And how can Courtine be so astonished by the drawing of a relationship between the *es gibt* of Meinong and that of Heidegger in 1927 ("a preposterous idea," he writes, in Meinong, *Théorie de l'objet,* 34)?

39. Immanuel Kant, *Kritik der reinen Vernunft,* A290; *Critique of Pure Reason,* trans. Norman Kemp Smith (London: Macmillan, 1961), 294.

40. Edmund Husserl, *Ideen I,* §42, Hua. 3, 96; *Ideas Pertaining to a Pure Phenomenology and to a Phenomenological Philosophy, First Book: General Introduction to a Pure Phenomenology,* trans. F. Kersten (Dordrecht: Kluwer Academic Publishers, 1982), 90 (trans. modified). See §46, 109 (where the difference between *Erlebnis* and transcendence leads back to the difference between two *leibhaft Gegebene*), and the commentary of Didier Franck, *Chair et corps: Sur la phénoménologie de Husserl* (Paris: Editions de Minuit, 1981), 24ff.

41. Husserl did not fail to recognize the possibility, or indeed the obligation, of such an exit out, beyond being (see the light shed on this issue in Marion, *Réduction et donation; Reduction and Givenness,* §§1–7), but he essentially leaves it undecided.

2. Remarks on the Origins of *Gegebenheit* in Heidegger's Thought

This text corrects and modifies a study that appeared in tribute to a friend and eminent colleague, under the title "Ce que donne 'Cela donne,'" in *Le souci du passage: Mélanges offerts à Jean Greisch,* ed. Philippe Capelle, Geneviève Hébert, and Marie-Dominique Popelard (Paris: Cerf, 2004), 293–306.

1. Martin Heidegger, *Zur Bestimmung der Philosophie,* ed. Bernd Heim-

büchel, *Gesamtausgabe*, vol. 56/57 (Frankfurt a/M.: Vittorio Klostermann, 1987); *Towards the Definition of Philosophy*, trans. Ted Sadler (London: Continuum Books, 2008). Subsequent citations to the German edition will be given by the abbreviation *GA*, followed by volume, section, and page number; this will be followed by a reference to the English translation, abbreviated *TDP*.

2. Martin Heidegger, *Grundprobleme der Phänomenologie* (1919/20), *Anhang A*, ed. Hans-Helmuth Gander, in *GA* 58 (Frankfurt a./M.: Vittorio Klostermann, 1993), 131.

3. *Grundprobleme der Phänomenologie, GA* 58, §26, 127 (see p. 27).

4. *Grundprobleme der Phänomenologie, GA* 58, §1, 5. See: "The sphere of the problem of phenomenology is not simply immediately pre-given [. . .]. And what does it mean to say: something must be, mediately, first '*brought*' to givenness?" (§6, 27).

5. Jean Greisch (in *L'arbre de vie et l'arbre du savoir: Les racines phénoménologiques de l'herméneutique heidegerrienne [1991–1923]* [Paris: Cerf, 2000], 38) recalls judiciously that Theodore Kisiel mentions a student note that glosses this already enigmatic formula with another that is even more surprising: "Gibt es ein 'es gibt,' wenn nur 'es gibt' gibt?—Does it give an 'it gives,' if it only gives an 'it gives'?" (quoted in Kisiel, *The Genesis of Heidegger's* Being and Time [Berkeley: University of California Press, 1993], 42).

6. *Grundprobleme der Phänomenologie, GA* 58, §7, 29. The same formula is found in *Anhang B, Ergänzung 1*, p. 203 (see also pp. 218 and 219).

7. "Es 'muß der Gegebenheit ein aktives *Geben* entsprechen.'" Heidegger is here quoting Natorp's "Bruno Brauchs *Immanuel Kant* und die Fortbildung des System des kritischen Idealismus," *Kantstudien* 22 (1918): 440 (Heidegger, *GA* 56/57, §19, 106; *TDP* 81–82). The same argument appears in the book review "Husserls *Ideen zu einer reinen Phänomenologie,*" *Die Geisteswissenschaften* (1913), and later in *Logos* 7 (1917–18); French translation, accompanied by a very useful introduction, published by J. Servois, in *Philosophie* 74 (Paris: Editions de Minuit, 2002).

8. *Grundprobleme der Phänomenologie, Anhang B, 2, GA* 58, 132.

9. Ibid., 224 and 225.

10. Paul Natorp, *Allgemeine Psychologie nach kritischer Methode. I. Band: Objekt und Methode der Psychologie*, chap. 3, §1 (Tübingen: Verlag von J. C. B. Mohr, 1912), 40: "Auch ein 'Datum' der Psychologie kann das Ich der reinen Bewußtheit nicht eigentlich genannt werden. Datum hieße Problem; Problem aber ist das reine Ich eben nicht. Es ist Prinzip; ein Prinzip aber ist niemals 'gegeben,' sondern, je radikaler, um so ferner allem Gegebenen. 'Gegeben' würde überdies heißen 'Einem gegeben,' das aber hieße wiederum: Einem bewußt. Das Bewußt-sein ist im Begriff des Gegebenen also schon vorausgesetzt. Eben als Voraussetzung aller Gegebenheit kann

aber die reine Bewußtheit selbst nicht 'gegeben' heißen; so wie das Erscheinen selbst nicht eine Erscheinung." See also chap. 5, §16, 122.

11. *Allgemeine Psychologie,,* chap. 2, §5, 32: "[...] die paradoxe Konsequenz, daß das ursprüngliche, reine Ich, das Ich der Bewußtheit, [...] weder Tatsache noch Existierendes noch Phänomen ist. Aber die Paradoxie hebt sich auf, sobald man sich klar macht: es ist Grund aller Tatsache, Grund aller Existenz, alles Gegebenseins, alles Erscheinens; nur darum kann es selbst nicht eine Tatsache, eine Existenz, ein Gegebenes, ein Erscheinendes sein." See also chap. 4, §3, 66.

12. We can refer to the illuminating and detailed analysis of Theodore Kisiel, "Why Students of Heidegger Will Have to Read Emil Lask," *Man and World* 28 (1995): 197–240, included in Kisiel, *Heidegger's Way of Thought: Critical and Interpretive Signposts* (New York: Continuum, 2002), 101–36.

13. The *Grundprobleme der Phänomenologie* assimilates them clearly ("*Transzendentale Wertphilosophie [Rickert, Lask]," GA* 58, 133), even at times putting Rickert "unter de[n] Einfluß von *Lask*" and not the inverse (226). And yet, is it not the case that Rickert in fact dedicated *Der Gegenstand der Erkenntnis* to Lask?

14. *Grundprobleme der Phänomenologie, GA* 58, 133, which cites, or summarizes rather loosely, Rickert's *Der Gegenstand der Erkenntnis: Einführung in die Transzendentalphilosophie,* according to the third edition (Tübingen, 1915), 376 ff., or according to the fourth edition, which I will refer to here (Tübingen: Verlag von J. C. B. Mohr, 1921), 325 ff.

15. *Grundprobleme der Phänomenologie, GA* 58, 226, which doubtless refers to: "*Dies* Blau und *dies* Rot bleibt in jeder Hinsicht unableitbar oder, wie wir auch sagen können, *irrational,* denn an den bestimmten Inhalten findet alles 'Denken' seine Grenze" (*Der Gegenstand der Erkenntnis,* 326).

16. *Grundprobleme der Phänomenologie, GA* 58, 226.

17. *Der Gegenstand der Erkenntnis,* 327: "Farbe ist, heißt so viel wie: Farbe ist Tatsache, ist gegeben, ist wahrgenommen."

18. *Der Gegenstand der Erkenntnis,* 328: "die Form des *individuellen* real Gegebenen oder die Bejahungsform des Urteils, das ein rein tatsächliches, individuell bestimmtes *einmaliges* real Gegebenes konstatiert."

19. *Der Gegenstand der Erkenntnis,* 330: "es gibt zwar keine individuellen Formen und Normen, aber es gibt *Formen und Normen des Individuellen.*"

20. *Der Gegenstand der Erkenntnis,* 331: "die Kategorie des realen *Diesseins.*"

21. *Der Gegenstand der Erkenntnis,* 327 (cited by Heidegger, *GA* 58, 134); in fact Rickert writes: "auch die Tatsächlichkeit als *Kategorie* zu verstehen." Even here, Heidegger assimilates *Gegebenheit* to *Tatsächlichkeit,* beginning from the current formula of Rickert's, cited in the following note.

22. *Der Gegenstand der Erkenntnis,* chap. 5, s. III: "Die Kategorie der Gegebenheit," e.g., pp. 327 and 328: "*Kategorie der Gegebenheit oder Tatsächlichkeit.*"

23. *Grundprobleme der Phänomenologie, GA* 58, §15, 71.

24. *Grundprobleme der Phänomenologie, Anhang B, GA* 58, 131.

25. *Grundprobleme der Phänomenologie, Anhang B, GA* 58, 226 and 227.

26. Well before Sellars and Reichenbach, Natorp had already spoken of the "prejudice of the given [*Das Vorurteil des Gegebenen*]" (*Allgemeine Psychologie*, 278).

27. Confirmation is found in *Grundprobleme der Phänomenologie, Anhang B, GA* 58, 220, 223, 231. For life is structured like a language, its own: "Das Leben spricht zu sich selbst in seiner eigenen Sprache" (231, see also 31).

28. Martin Heidegger, *Zeit und Sein*, in *Zur Sache des Denkens* (Tübingen: Niemeyer, 1969), 23; *On Time and Being*, trans. Joan Stambaugh (New York: Harper and Row, 1972), 22 (trans. modified). See my study of this point in *Étant donné: Essai d'une phénoménologie de la donation* (Paris: Presses Universitaires de France, 1997, 1998), §3, 54–60; *Being Given: Toward a Phenomenology of Givenness*, trans. Jeffrey L. Kosky (Stanford, CA: Stanford University Press, 2002), 34–39.

3. Substitution and Solicitude

1. Paul Ricoeur, "Emmanuel Lévinas, penseur du témoignage" (1989), in Ricoeur, *Lectures 3: Aux frontières de la philosophie* (Paris: Seuil, 1994), 99, 100.

2. Emmanuel Lévinas, "Un Dieu Homme?," in *Entre nous: Essais sur le penser-à-l'autre* (Paris: Editions Grasset & Fasquelle, 1991), 76 (my emphasis); *Entre nous: On thinking-of-the-other*, trans. Michael B. Smith and Barbara Harshav (New York: Columbia University Press, 1998), 60.

3. Emmanuel Lévinas, *Autrement qu'être ou au-delà de l'essence* (The Hague: Martinus Nijhoff, 1974), 152; *Otherwise than Being or Beyond Essence*, trans. Alphonso Lingis (Pittsburgh: Duquesne University Press, 1981, 1997), 119.

4. *Autrement qu'être*, 127; trans. Lingis, 100.

5. *Autrement qu'être*, 141; trans. Lingis, 111.

6. And it seems that such is indeed the case, at least according to *Entre nous*, 262; trans. Smith and Harshav, 231.

7. *Autrement qu'être*, 141; trans. Lingis, 111.

8. *Autrement qu'être*, v; trans. Lingis, v.

9. *Autrement qu'être*, 152 and 232, respectively; trans. Lingis 119 and 184 (trans. modified).

10. Emmanuel Lévinas, *Ethique et infini: Dialogues avec Philippe Nemo* (Paris: Librairie Arthème Fayard/Radio France, 1982), 95–96; *Ethics and Infinity: Conversations with Philippe Nemo*, trans. Richard A. Cohen (Pittsburgh: Duquesne University Press, 1985), 90. See "It is in a *responsibility that is justified by no prior commitment*, in the responsibility for another—in an ethical situation—that the me-ontological and metalogical structure of this anarchy takes form" (*Autrement qu'être*, 129; trans. Lingis, 102). Or, we

must understand ethics itself in an extra-moral sense: "The ethical is not a region or an ornament of the real, it is of itself disinterestedness itself, which is only possible under the traumatism in which presence, in its impenitent equanimity of presence, is upset by the Other" (*Nouvelles lectures talmudiques* [Paris: Editions de Minuit, 1996], 34; *New Talmudic Readings*, trans. Richard A. Cohen [Pittsburgh: Duquesne University Press, 1999], 70). This is confirmed by a declaration of Levinas's, reported by Jacques Derrida: "You know, one often speaks of ethics to describe what I do, but what really interests me in the end is not ethics, not ethics alone, but the holy, the holiness of the holy" (Derrida, *Adieu à Emmanuel Lévinas* [Paris: Editions Galilée, 1997], 15; *Adieu to Emmanuel Levinas*, trans. Pascale-Anne Brault and Michael Naas [Stanford, CA: Stanford University Press, 1999], 4).

11. Emmanuel Lévinas, *De Dieu qui vient à l'idée* (Paris: Vrin, 1992), 228; *Of God Who Comes to Mind*, trans. Bettina Bergo (Stanford, CA: Stanford University Press, 1998), 149. I follow here Jacques Rolland's excellent commentary: "'ethics' (which thus must not be taken as a feminine substantive but, instead, if the word were not itself problematic, ought to be understood as the ethical (order) [*l'(ordre) éthique*], with a masculine that is perhaps capable of recalling the neutral of the German substantivized adjective [*das Ethische*]) *is not a discipline*—and [. . . so], already for this reason, its term-for-term opposition with 'ontology' obviously proceeds not without raising problems" (*Parcours de l'Autrement: Lecture d'Emmanuel Lévinas* [Paris: Presses Universitaires de France, 2000], 17).

12. That is, insofar as ethics forms a group with logic and physics in the Stoic classification, or, in modern scholasticism, makes up a system with metaphysics, logic, and physics under the name of *ethics or moral philosophy* [*l'éthique ou philosophie morale*] (chosen as a title by S. Dupleix [Paris, 1610]; see also the *Summa quadripartita, de rebus dialecticis, Moralibus, Physicis et Metaphysicis*, by E. de Saint-Paul [Paris, 1609]). Jacques Rolland, once again, insists: "Thus is the meaning of ethics articulated. Once again, one must not understand it beginning from some moral or, even worse, moralizing prejudice. What comes into question here is nothing other than what we might call the 'constitution of the ego [*moi*],' the genesis of its ipseity and of its un-ity" (preface to Emmanuel Lévinas, *Ethique comme philosophie première* [Paris: Payot, 1998], 46).

13. *Autrement qu'être*, 163; trans. Lingis, 127.

14. "This is why Heidegger seems to me to dominate from above the philosophy of existence, despite the deepening or modification that one might bring to the content of his analyses. One can be to him what Malebranche or Spinoza had been to Descartes. It's not too shabby, but it's not Descartes' destiny" (Emmanuel Lévinas, *En découvrant l'existence avec Husserl et Heidegger* [Paris: Vrin, 1949, 1974], 101). Or: "Despite all the horror that eventually came to be associated with Heidegger's name—and which will never

be dissipated—nothing has been able to destroy in my mind the conviction that the *Sein und Zeit* of 1927 cannot be annulled, no more than can the few other eternal books in the history of philosophy" (*Entre-nous*, 220, see also 134 and 255; trans. Smith and Harshav, 208, see also 116 and 225).

15. In "Mourir pour . . . ," a lecture given at the Collège International de Philosophie in Paris, March 1987, collected in *Entre nous*, 219–30; trans. Smith and Harshav, "Dying for . . . ," 207–17. I would like here to deepen an hypothesis suggested by Robert Bernasconi, "What Is the Question to Which Substitution Is the Answer?," in *The Cambridge Companion to Levinas*, ed. Simon Critchley and Robert Bernasconi (Cambridge: Cambridge University Press, 2002), 234–51.

16. "Auf dem Grunde dieses *mithaften* In-der-Welt-seins ist die Welt je schon immer die, die ich mit den Anderen teile. Die Welt des Daseins ist *Mitwelt*. Das In-Sein ist *Mitsein* mit Anderen. Das innerweltliche Ansichsein dieser ist *Mitdasein*" (Martin Heidegger, *Sein und Zeit*, §26 [Tübingen: Max Niemeyer Verlag, 1996], 118; *Being and Time: A Translation of "Sein und Zeit,"* trans. Joan Stambaugh [Albany: State University of New York Press, 1996], 111–12).

17. "Das eigene Dasein ist nur, sofern es die Wesensstruktur des Mitseins hat, als für Andere begegnend Mitdasein" (*Sein und Zeit*, 121; trans. Stambaugh, 113).

18. I must admit that I do not understand why Stambaugh in her recent American translation of *Sein und Zeit* chose to render *Fürsorge* by "welfare work" (114ff.), thus losing any link to *Sorge/cura/*care.

19. Of course, Levinas calls attention to and contests this treatment of solicitude in "Dying for . . . ," *Entre nous*, trans. Smith and Harshav, 212 ff.

20. Emmanuel Lévinas, *Du sacré au saint: Cinq nouvelles lectures talmudiques* (Paris: Editions de Minuit, 1977), 16; *Nine Talmudic Readings*, trans. Annette Aronowicz (Bloomington: Indiana University Press, 1990, 1994), 97. Put another way, according to "the saying of the Lithuanian rabbi Israel Salanter: the material needs of my neighbor are my spiritual needs" (20; trans. Aronowicz, 99).

21. On the blurring of the identity and the own-ness of the other, or indeed his anonymity, in the gift, see my analysis in §9 of *Étant donné: Essai d'une phénoménologie de la donation* (Paris: Presses Universitaires de France, 1996, 2005), 124ff.; *Being Given*, trans. Jeffrey L. Kosky (Stanford, CA: Stanford University Press, 2002), 85–94.

22. *Sein und Zeit*, §26, 122, line 3; trans. Stambaugh, 114. The same analysis is found in Heidegger's *Logik: Die Frage nach der Wahrheit, GA* 21, §9, 224.

23. *Sein und Zeit*, §26, 122, lines 5 ff. (the exact same terms are found in *Logik*, §8, 225). The French translation (by E. Martineau) does not hesitate to translate *einspringen* by "se *substituer* à lui" (105). This choice forces the

feature a bit (it is a question of "leaping in place of someone") and would fit better with "sich an seine Stelle setzen," but it does signal well that the issue is indeed one of substitution.

24. *Sein und Zeit*, §26, 122, line 10; see *Logik*, §9, 2 *(Herrschaft, Beherrschte, beherrschende Fürsorge)*. This is a transparent allusion to G. W. F. Hegel's *Phänomenologie des Geistes*, IV, A, ed. J. Hoffmeister (Hamburg: Felix Meiner Verlag, 1952), 141 ff.; Hegel, *Phenomenology of Spirit*, trans. A. V. Miller (New York: Oxford University Press, 1977), 111 ff.

25. " . . . die für den Anderen nicht so sehr einspringt, als daß sie ihm in seinem existenziellen Seinskönnen *vorausspringt*, nicht um ihm die 'Sorge' abzunehmen, sondern erst eigentlich als solche zurückzugeben" *(Sein und Zeit*, §26, 122, lines 16–20; trans. Stambaugh, 115). The parallel passage in *Logik* speaks of "zwei extreme Modi der Fürsorge, die eigentliche und die uneigentliche" (224).

26. *Sein und Zeit*, §29, 134, line 23; trans. Stambaugh, 127. In opposition to the *They (On)*, which discharges the burden *(Entlastung*, §27, 127, line 39, and §54, 268, line 6).

27. *Sein und Zeit*, §26, 122, line 5.

28. "daß es je sein Sein als seiniges zu sein hat" *(Sein und Zeit*, §4, 12, line 23; trans. Stambaugh, 10).

29. "Zum existierenden Dasein gehört die Jemeinigkeit als Bedingung der Möglichkeit von Eigentlichkeit und Uneigentlichkeit" *(Sein und Zeit*, §12, 53, lines 3–5; trans. Stambaugh, 49). As for giving a moral interpretation to *Jemeinigkeit* and understanding it as an exclusive possession of its being— supposing that Levinas indeed thus understands it—one could doubt that it would draw much in the way of consequences, precisely because, for Heidegger, it is never anything other than a strict ontological determination: "Am Sterben zeigt sich, daß der Tod ontologisch durch Jemeinigkeit und Existenz konstituiert wird." (In dying, it becomes evident that death is ontologically constituted by mineness and existence.) *(Sein und Zeit*, §47, 240, lines 13–14; trans. Stambaugh, 223).

30. Not *for* but *toward* death, following an explicit remark of Heidegger's: "serious errors can become doubly rooted, like the one that has been spread because of the first French translations—and which it is currently almost no longer possible to eradicate—namely, the translation of the locution, "*Sein zum Tode*" by *being-for-death*, rather than *being-toward-death*" *(Lettres à Hannah Arendt*, April 21, 1954, in Hannah Arendt and Martin Heidegger, *Lettres et autres documents, 1925–1975*, ed. Ursula Ludz, French trans. Pascal David [Paris: Gallimard, 2001], 139). Jacques Derrida comments, "Decease [*Anleben*] is not dying but, as we saw, only a being-for-death [*Dasein*], a being-pledged-to-death, a being-to-death or tensed-toward-(or as far as)-death [*zum Tode*] is able also to *decease*" *(Apories* [Paris: Galilée, 1996], 76; see also 102).

31. "Der Tod ist eine Seinsmöglichkeit, die je das Dasein selbst zu über-nehmen hat"; and "*Keiner kann dem Anderen sein Sterben abnehmen*" (*Sein und Zeit*, §50, 250, lines 29–30, and §47, 240, lines 4–5, respectively; trans. Stambaugh 232 and 223).

32. *Sein und Zeit*, §51, 253, lines 19–20; trans. Stambaugh 234.

33. "So enthüllt sich der *Tod* als *die eigenste, unbezügliche, unüberholbare Möglichkeit*" (*Sein und Zeit*, §50, 250; see §52, 258, lines 38 ff., which com-pletes the description with "*gewisse und als solche unbestimmte*," "*the ownmost nonrelational, certain, and, as such, indefinite and not to be bypassed possibility*" (trans. Stambaugh, 239).

34. Martin Heidegger, *Prolegomena zur Geschichte des Zeitbegriffs* (1925), *GA* 20, 437 ff.

35. *Sein und Zeit*, §51, 253, line 37; trans. Stambaugh, 235. It is no coin-cidence that "*Fürsorge*" reappears here (line 34). When we "are [. . .] just 'there'" (§47, 239, line 6; trans. Stambaugh, 222) at the moment of another's death, rather than accomplishing the least substitution, we experience in this very proximity that it remains unthinkable. All that remains, in this powerlessness, is to "console" (§51, 254, line 1; trans. Stambaugh, 235: "tranquilization"), at best in the sense of a "dominating" solicitude.

36. "Zu den Seinsmöglichkeiten des Miteinanderseins in der Welt gehört unstreitig die *Vertretbarkeit* des einen Daseins durch ein anderes" (*Sein und Zeit*, §47, 239, line 24; trans. Stambaugh, 223).

37. "Das Sterben, das wesenhaft unvertretbar das meine ist, wird in ein öffentlich vorkommendes Ereignis verkehrt, das dem Man begegnet" (*Sein und Zeit*, §51, 253, lines 19–21; trans. Stambaugh, 234, modified).

38. "Sorge ist immer, wenn auch nur privativ, Besorgen und Fürsorge" (*Sein und Zeit*, §41, 194, line 23; trans. Stambaugh, 181).

39. "[. . .] die besorgende Fürsorge" (*Sein und Zeit*, §53, 266, line 15; trans. Stambaugh, 245: "concern taking care of things").

40. Husserl hesitated to decide whether the other would offer only "ein-fach ein Duplikat meiner selbst" (*Cartesianische Meditationen*, §43, Hua. 1, 146), or instead another center, irrevocably decentered from my own. Hei-degger, for his part, shows no hesitation: he concedes to the other's alter-ity only the repetition of the originary unsubstitutability of ipseity: "Der Andere ist eine Dublette des Selbst" (*Sein und Zeit*, §26, 124, line 36; trans. Stambaugh, 117: "The other is a double of the self").

41. *Autrement qu'être*, 185; trans. Lingis, 145.

42. Emmanuel Lévinas, *Difficile liberté: Essais sur le judaïsme* (Paris: Albin Michel, 1963, 1994), 120; *Difficult Freedom: Essays on Judaism*, trans. Seán Hand (Baltimore: Johns Hopkins University Press, 1990), 89. The "burden imposed by the suffering of others" here replaces the "burden of being" (see n. 26 above).

43. *Autrement qu'être*, 130; trans. Lingis, 102.

44. *Autrement qu'être,* 151; trans. Lingis, 118 (with a correction: Lingis translates "voluntary" for the French "involontaire").

45. *Autrement qu'être,* 61 and 142; trans. Lingis, 47 and 111; see too 180 (trans. Lingis, 141), or *De Dieu qui vient à l'idée,* 167; trans. Bergo, 106.

46. *Autrement qu'être,* 128; trans. Lingis, 101.

47. For a nonstandard interpretation of the *cogito,* see Jean-Luc Marion, "L'altérité originaire de l'*ego—Meditation II,* AT VII, 24–25," *Questions Cartésiennes II* (Paris: Presses Universitaires de France, 1996), 3–47; *On the Ego and God: Further Cartesian Questions,* trans. Christina M. Gschwandtner (New York: Fordham University Press, 2007), 3–29.

48. *Autrement qu'être,* 159; trans. Lingis, 124.

49. *Autrement qu'être,* 180; trans. Lingis, 142.

50. *Autrement qu'être,* 69; trans. Lingis, 53.

51. According to Rodolphe Calin's very accurate analysis, *Lévinas et l'exception du soi* (Paris: Presses Universitaires de France, 2005), 138. Indeed, I never appear for myself, and thus by myself: everyone can see my face, except me, who only sees it reversed in a mirror. Strictly speaking, each person remains invisible (non-intendable, *invisable*) to himself and must, in order to see himself, make himself seen, in order to appear and to appear before [others], submitting the care of his appearing to the gaze of the other.

52. *Autrement qu'être,* 107; trans. Lingis, 85 (emphasis added).

53. *Sein und Zeit,* §57, 277, line 31 and 275, line 13, respectively; trans. Stambaugh, 256 and 254.

54. *Autrement qu'être,* 150; trans. Lingis, 117 (emphasis added) (see *Entre nous,* 76; trans. Smith and Harshav, 60, cited above in n. 2).

55. *Nouvelles lectures talmudiques,* 20; trans. Cohen, 58.

56. *Autrement qu'être,* 151; trans. Lingis, 118.

57. *Autrement qu'être,* 146 and 150, respectively; trans. Lingis, 114 and 117.

58. *Autrement qu'être,* 148; trans. Lingis 116: "without any choice"; 151, trans. Lingis, 118 (corrected): "involuntary, [. . .] prior to the will's initiative"; 186, trans. Lingis 146: "before all freedom."

59. "The subject is in the accusative, without recourse in being" (*Autrement qu'être,* 140; trans. Lingis, 110). See "Responsibility for the other is extraordinary, and is not prevented from floating over the waters of ontology" (180; trans. Lingis, 141).

60. *Autrement qu'être,* 142; trans. Lingis, 112 (emphasis added).

61. *Autrement qu'être,* 163; trans. Lingis 127 (trans. modified) (see "This book interprets the *subject* as a *hostage,*" 232, trans. Lingis, 184, cited above in n. 9).

62. *Autrement qu'être,* 146; trans. Lingis, 115 (trans. modified). See: "*one* absolved from every relationship, every game, literally without a situation,

without a dwelling place, expelled from everywhere and from itself" (189; trans. Lingis, 146).

63. *Autrement qu'être*, 150; trans. Lingis, 117 (trans. modified).

64. *Autrement qu'être*, 145; trans. Lingis, 114.

65. *Autrement qu'être*, 173; trans. Lingis, 135. We must not misunderstand by seeing here the definition of racism (to accuse the other of *being* what he is, so that he is not allowed any escape), because here (a) the point is not the accusing of the other, but *my* responsibility; and above all because here (b) I discover myself accused not of my being but even *before* being—before being *(l'être)*, and from elsewhere.

66. *Autrement qu'être*, 143; trans. Lingis, 112.

67. *Autrement qu'être*, 196; trans. Lingis, 153 (emphasis added, trans. modified). Rodolphe Calin says it well: "What isolates me is my responsibility for the death of the other, and not for my own death" *(Lévinas et l'exception du soi*, 290). "Isolates" here naturally translates both the *entelekheia* of the act in Aristotle, *Metaphysics Z*, 13.1039a7, and the *vereinzeln* of *Sein und Zeit*, §40, 188, line 18.

68. *Autrement qu'être*, 149; trans. Lingis, 117 (emphasis added).

69. *Autrement qu'être*, 177; trans. Lingis, 139 (emphasis added, trans. modified).

70. "Die *Selbst-ständigkeit* bedeutet existenzial nichts anderes als die vorlaufende Entschlossenheit" *(Sein und Zeit*, §64, 322, line 37; trans. Stambaugh, 297).

71. *Autrement qu'être*, 151; trans. Lingis, 118.

72. *Autrement qu'être*, 143; trans. Lingis, 112.

73. *Difficile liberté*, 247; trans. Hand, 190. See: "Israel would teach that the greatest intimacy of me to myself consists in being at every moment responsible for the others, the hostage of others. *I can be responsible for that which I did not do and take upon myself a distress which is not mine*" *(Du sacré au saint*, 181; trans. Aronowicz, 85).

74. "Dying for . . . ," in *Entre nous*, 229; trans. Smith and Harshav, 217.

75. *Autrement qu'être*, 163; trans. Lingis, 127 (trans. modified).

4. Sketch of a Phenomenological Concept of Sacrifice

This essay responds in certain ways to my earlier "Esquisse d'un concept phénoménologique du don," which appeared in *Filosofia della rivelazione*, ed. M. M. Olivetti (Rome: Biblioteca dell' *Archivio di Filosofia*, 1994); "Sketch of a Phenomenological Concept of the Gift," trans. John Conley, SJ, and Danielle Poe, in *Postmodern Philosophy and Christian Thought*, ed. Merold Westphal (Bloomington: Indiana University Press, 1999), 122–43; also published in English in Jean-Luc Marion, *The Visible and the Revealed*, trans. Christina M. Gschwandtner (New York: Fordham University Press, 2008), 80–100.

1. The same goes for anyone who puts his life in danger, ultimately for nothing, or almost nothing (the "adventurer" or the so-called extreme athlete). The question arises, at what point does such a figure, mundane as it appears, correspond—as its modern heir—to the figure of the master in the dialectic of recognition (the slave remaining within the domain of the profane, where he does not destroy himself)?

2. This was moreover the classical argument (forged by the Reformation, then taken up by the Enlightenment) against a peaceful but also radical figure of sacrifice—monastic vows: to renounce power, riches, and reproduction amounts to destroying goods, which allow the world to live and to increase, and this renunciation even makes one enter into the field of the sacred, in this case into a life that, if it is not outside the world, is at least oriented eschatalogically toward the alteration of this world.

3. The attempts to define sacrifice made by Henri Hubert and Marcel Mauss in the famous *Essai sur la nature et la fonction du sacrifice* (published first in the *Année sociologique* in 1898, then in Marcel Mauss, *Oeuvres*, ed. Victor Karady, vol. 1: *Les fonctions sociales du sacré* [Paris: Minuit, 1968]; *Sacrifice: Its Nature and Function*, trans. W. D. Halls [Chicago: University of Chicago Press, 1964]) are characterized by their poverty and their silence on the central (in fact the only) problem of the function and the intrinsic logic of sacrifice (its signification, its intention, its mechanism of compensation, etc.), contrasting all the more with the wealth of details on the actual practice of sacrifice. So if we suppose that "[s]acrifice [. . .] was originally a gift made by the primitive [*sic*] to supernatural forces to which he must bind himself" (193; trans. Halls, 2, modified), it remains to be understood whether and how these "forces" tolerate being thus "bound." The same abstraction and the same insufficiency obtain in the definition that is ultimately adopted: "Thus we finally arrive at the following definition: *Sacrifice is a religious act which, through the consecration of a victim, modifies the condition of the moral person who accomplishes it or that of certain objects with which he is concerned*" (205; trans. Halls, 13): what does "consecration" here signify? How is the person in question "modified"? When is it a matter of "objects" more than of him, and which objects? And, indeed, in what sense can or must this act be called "religious"? Who or what allows the "modification" in question? No response is given, because the questions are not even raised. These extraordinary approximations lead back inevitably to the features, themselves already highly imprecise, of the Maussian concept of the gift. (a) Sacrifice becomes a reciprocal gift that won't acknowledge itself as such: "If on the other hand, one seeks to bind the divinity by a contract, the sacrifice has rather the form of an attribution: *do ut des* is the principle" (272; trans. Halls, 65–66, modified); but what does it mean to bind "contractually" a "divinity" that has precisely the characteristic of being able to recuse

itself from any contract and any reciprocity? (b) The destruction is assumed to be effective by itself and, without further consideration, it is assimilated to the accomplished sacrifice without recognizing that at best it fulfils only one of its conditions, but not the principle one (acceptance of the gift by the divinity): "*This procedure* [the sacrifice!] *consists in establishing a line of communication between the sacred and the profane worlds through the mediation of a victim, that is, of a thing that in the course of the ceremony is destroyed*" (302; trans. Halls, 97); but who cannot see that the difficulty of such a "line of communication" consists precisely in the fact that the "sacred world" has no reason to accept it unless one can explain how the contrary could be the case? (c) Thus one ends by granting that the sacrifice, in the end, isn't one: "The sacrifier gives up something of himself but he does not give himself. Prudently, he sets himself aside. This is because if he gives, it is partly in order to receive" (304; trans. Halls, 100). One can hardly avoid reading this conclusion as an admission of failure to supply a rigorous definition of sacrifice.

4. Jacques Derrida, *Donner le temps. 1: la fausse monnaie* (Paris: Galilée 1991), 42; *Given Time: 1. Counterfeit Money*, trans. Peggy Kamuf (Chicago: University of Chicago Press, 1992), 27.

5. See Jean-Luc Marion, *Étant donné: Essai d'une phénoménologie de la donation*, §§9–11 (Paris: Presses Universitaires de France, 1997, 1998), 124–61; *Being Given: Toward a Phenomenology of Givenness*, trans. Jeffrey L. Kosky (Stanford, CA: Stanford University Press, 2002), 85–113; and, to begin, Marion, "Esquisse d'un concept phénoménologique du don" (cited above, unnumbered note).

6. "Quemadmodum, fratres, si sponsus faceret sponsae suae annulum, et illa acceptum annulum plus diligeret quam sponsum qui illi fecit annulum, none in ipso dono sponsi adultera anima deprehenderetur, quamvis hoc amaret quod dedit sponsus? Certe hoc amaret quod dedit sponsus; tamen si diceret: Sufficit mihi annulus iste, iam illius faciem nolo videre, qualis esset? Quis non detestaretur hanc amentiam? Quis non adulterinum animum convinceret? Amas aurum pro viro, amas annulum pro sponso; si hoc est in te, ut ames annulum pro sponso tuo, et nolis videre sponsum tuum, ad hoc tibi arrham dedit, ut non te oppigneraret, sed averteret" (St. Augustine, *In Epistulam Primam Iohannis Tractatus*, 2.11; English translation available in *The Fathers of the Church: St. Augustine, Tractates on the Gospel of John 112–24, Tractates on the First Epistle of John*, trans. John W. Rettig [Washington, DC: Catholic University of America Press, 1995], 154).

7. Martin Heidegger, *Zeit und Sein*, in *Zur Sache des Denkens*, in *GA* 14 (Frankfurt a./M.: Vittorio Klostermann, 2007), 12; *On Time and Being*, trans. Joan Stambaugh (New York: Harper and Row, 1972), 8.

8. Martin Heidegger, *Die onto-theo-logische Verfassung der Metaphysik*, in *Identität und Differenz*, in *GA* 11 (Frankfurt a./M.: Vittorio Klostermann,

2006), 71; *The Onto-theological Constitution of Metaphysics*, in *Identity and Difference*, trans. Joan Stambaugh (Chicago: University of Chicago Press, 2002), 64–65 (trans. modified).

9. Let us recall that we are dealing here with the three marks of the phenomenon as given (see *Étant donné*, §13, 170–71; *Being Given*, 119–20).

10. See the analysis of Roland de Vaux, *Les sacrifices de l'Ancien Testament* (Paris: J. Gabalda, 1964). In another sense, if one grants Ishmael the status of true firstborn, though born of a slave, he too is found rendered unto God by the sending into the desert (Genesis 21:9 ff.).

11. I translate Genesis 18:14 following the version of the Septuagint (μὴ ἀδυνατῆσεῖ παρὰ τῷ θεῷ ῥῆμα), in conformity with Luke 1:37, which quotes it οὐκ ἀδυνατῆσεῖ παρὰ τῷ θεῷ πᾶν ῥῆμα.

12. The death of the Christ accomplishes a sacrifice in *this* sense (more than in the common sense): by returning his spirit to the Father, who gives it to him, Jesus prompts the veil of the Temple (which separates God from men and makes him invisible to them) to be torn, and at once appears himself as "truly the son of God" (Matt. 27:51, 54), thus making appear not himself, but the invisible Father. The gift given thus allows both the giver and the process (here Trinitarian) of givenness to be seen. See my sketch in Jean-Luc Marion, "La reconnaissance du don," *Revue Catholique International Communio*, 33/1, no. 195 (January–February 2008).

13. Georges Bataille, *Théorie de la religion*, in *Oeuvres complètes*, vol. 7 (Paris: Gallimard, 1976), 310; *Theory of Religion*, trans. Robert Hurley (New York: Zone Books, 1989), 48–49 (trans. modified). More explicitly, Josef Ratzinger writes: "Christian sacrifice does not consist in a giving of what God would not have without us but in our becoming totally receptive and letting ourselves be completely taken over by him. Letting God act on us— that is Christian sacrifice. [. . .] In this form of worship human achievements are not placed before God; on the contrary, it consists in man's letting himself be endowed with gifts" (*Introduction to Christianity*, trans. J. R. Foster [San Francisco: Ignatius Press, 1990, 2004], 283).

14. Emmanuel Lévinas, "Enigme et phénomène," in *En découvrant l'existence avec Husserl et Heidegger* (Paris: Vrin, 1949, 1974), 215; "Enigma and Phenomenon," trans. Alphonso Lingis, in *Emmanuel Levinas: Basic Philosophical Writings*, ed. Adriaan T. Peperzak, Simon Critchley, and Robert Bernasconi (Bloomington: Indiana University Press, 1996), 77.

15. Jan Patočka, "The Dangers of Technicization in Science According to E. Husserl and the Essence of Technology as Danger According to M. Heidegger" (1973), in Erazim V. Kohák, *Jan Patočka: Philosophy and Selected Writings* (Chicago: University of Chicago Press, 1989), 332 (trans. modified in light of the French translation: Patočka, *Liberté et sacrifice: Écrits politiques*, trans. Erika Abrams [Grenoble: Jérôme Millon, 1990], 266). On this question, see the work of Emilie Tardivel, "Transcendance et liberté: Lévinas,

Patočka et la question du mal," *Cahiers d'Études Lévinassiennes*, no. 7 (March 2008): 155–75.

16. Saint Augustine, *De civitate dei*, 10.6, Bibliothèque Augustinienne, vol. 34, 446; *The City of God Against the Pagans*, trans. R. W. Dyson (Cambridge: Cambridge University Press, 1998), 400. See St. Thomas Aquinas: "omne opus virtutis dicitur esse sacrificium, inquantum ordinatur ad Dei reverentiam" (*Summa theologiae IIa–IIae*, q.81, a.4, *ad* 1).

Index

89; as mode of phenomenality, 19–20, 25; of non-sense, contradiction, and nothingness, 29–30; phenomenology of, 2, 3, 5–6, 7, 8, 11, 12, 14, 16, 17, 49, 99n30; self-, 3, 12, 14, 34; translation of, 19–20, 82, 96n2

giver *(donateur)*, 76–79, 82, 84–85, 88–90

God, 67, 85–89, 90; death of, 69

Greisch, Jean, 101n5

guilt, 61, 62–63, 64

Hart, Kevin, 2

Hegel, G. F., 56, 110n1

Heidegger, Martin, 1, 2, 3, 7, 8, 9, 10, 17, 20, 21, 27, 32, 34, 35, 38, 50, 61, 65, 68, 90, 107n40; *Kriegsnotsemester* 1919 course of, 7, 21, 35–37, 38–39, 41–49; 1919–20 course of, 39, 40; *Sein und Zeit*, 21–25, 27, 33–34, 48, 53–59, 67, 81; *Zeit und Sein*, 21, 24, 49, 80–81

Henry, Michel, 96n1

hermeneutics 13–14, 21, 78

Husserl, Edmund, 2, 3, 7, 8, 9, 20, 27, 32, 33, 34, 94n17, 95n19, 99n30, 100n41, 107n40; *The Idea of Phenomenology*, 28–30; *Ideas*, 33

"I," the, 3, 27, 28, 29, 38–39, 43–44, 47, 49, 51, 59–66, 67, 68

impossible, the, 29–31, 32, 33, 57, 59, 80, 86

infinite, the, 51, 59–60, 90, 96n27

intentionality, 59

intuition, 3, 4; conceptual structure of, 10

ipseity, 53, 58–59, 64–66, 67

Isaac, 85–89

Ishmael, 112n10

"it gives"/*es gibt*, 21–26, 27, 30, 32, 33, 34, 35–37, 40, 42–49, 80–81, 90; translation of, 22, 97n7, 97n9

Jesus Christ, 112n12

justice, 52

Kant, Immanuel, 32, 34

Kisiel, Theodore, 101n5, 102n12

Lask, Emil, 2, 25, 28–29, 32, 39, 98n20

Levinas, Emmanuel, 1, 17, 50–53, 56, 68, 90; commentary on *Sein und Zeit*, 53, 67, 104n14; *Otherwise than Being*, 50–52, 59–67

Lewis, Stephen E., 96n27

Locke, John, 5

looks/looking, 15, 16–17

love, 67, 96n27

Luke, references to book of: 1:37, 112n11

Mach, Ernst, 9

Mackinlay, Shane, 13–17, 92n7

Marburg school, 8, 9, 11, 39, 94n18

Marion, Jean-Luc: "The Banality of Saturation," 4, 93n9; *Being Given*, 2, 3, 5; *Certitudes négatives*, 3, 4, 93n11; *The Erotic Phenomenon*, 96n27; on givenness, 6; and history of philosophy, 2, 4, 5; *In Excess*, 3; phenomenological project of, 1, 2; *The Reason of the Gift*, 1, 2, 5, 7–8, 11; *Reduction and Givenness*, 2

Matthew, references to book of: 27:51, 54, 112n12

McDowell, John, 2, 5, 6, 7, 10, 11,
12, 13, 15, 91n1, 94nn17–18,
95n20; *Mind and World*, 5, 9,
13
Meinong, Alexius, 2, 7, 20, 30–32,
33
metaphysics, 8, 20, 22, 24, 25, 30,
31–32, 33, 46–47, 52, 62, 65,
104n12; *causa sui* in, 80
mineness *(Jemeinigkeit)*, 57–59, 65,
68, 106n29
monasticism, 110n2
morality, 61, 62, 66

Natorp, Paul, 2, 7, 8, 9, 21, 27,
28–29, 32, 33, 38–40, 41, 103n26
neo-Kantianism, 2, 4, 6, 7, 8, 9,
10–12, 13, 27, 32, 94nn17–18,
95n20; and conception of givenness, 8, 9–10, 13, 34, 42
Neurath, Otto, 5, 19
nihilism, 69
nonobjective thought, 2, 4, 11
Numbers, references to book of:
18:14, 86

object, the, 26, 27, 30, 31–32,
33–34, 39, 43, 44–47, 48–49, 78,
82, 84; constitution of, 4, 38,
46–47, 48; in general (Kant), 32,
33, 40; intentional, 28; present-
to-hand *(vorhanden)*, 27; theory
of, 7, 27, 31–32
objectifying thought, 7, 8, 38
objectivity, 3, 47
ontological difference, 23, 80
ontology, 25, 26, 27, 31–32, 33, 34,
40, 43, 52, 57, 65, 81
onto-theology, 20
other, the, 51, 52, 53–54, 55, 58–59,
60–61, 63–66, 67, 105n21,

107n40; as co-*Dasein*, 54–57; in
relation to sacrifice, 72–75
Other, the, 56

Patočka, Jan, 90
Peacocke, Christopher, 94n17
persecutor, the/persecution, 50–51,
63
phenomenality, 12–13, 14, 19, 20,
32, 39, 47, 60, 81, 82–85
phenomenology, 5, 6, 7, 9, 11–13,
20, 25, 34, 36–37, 39, 41, 42, 44,
49, 51, 52, 60, 68, 79, 81, 84,
85
presence-to-hand/*Vorhandenheit*,
22, 26
profane, 69–71

racism, 109n65
ready-to-hand/*zuhanden*, 70–71
reason, 52, 63, 65, 70;
nonreciprocal, 17
recipient *(donataire)*, 76, 84, 89–90
reciprocity, 74–75, 76, 77, 96n27,
110n3. *See also* exchange; sacrifice, according to exchange
reduction: metaphysical, 24; phenomenological, 2, 3, 28, 33, 44,
66, 76, 82, 83–85, 87–89, 90
reference, phenomenal structure of
(Hinweis), 79
Reformation, the, 110n2
Reichenbach, Hans, 103n26
responsibility, 50–51, 62–66, 68,
103n10, 109n73
revenge, 51
Rickert, Heinrich, 2, 7, 8, 21, 26,
28–29, 32, 38, 39–40, 41
Ricoeur, Paul, 50
Rolland, Jacques, 104n11
Romano, Claude, 7; *Au coeur de*

Page-Barbour and Richard Lectures
(IN PRINT)

SIR JOHN SUMMERSON
The Architecture of Victorian London

JOHANNES FABIAN
Moments of Freedom: Anthropology and Popular Culture

IAN HACKING
Mad Travelers: Reflections on the Reality of Transient Mental Illnesses

HARVIE FERGUSON
Modernity and Subjectivity: Body, Soul, Spirit

STEPHEN MULHALL
The Conversation of Humanity

FREEMAN J. DYSON
A Many-Colored Glass: Reflections on the Place of Life in the Universe

MAURICE GODELIER
In and Out of the West: Reconstructing Anthropology
Translated by Nora Scott

RICHARD J. SMITH
Fathoming the Cosmos and Ordering the World: The "Yijing"
("I Ching," or "Classic of Changes") and Its Evolution in China

MARTIN JAY
The Virtues of Mendacity: On Lying in Politics

JEAN-LUC MARION
The Reason of the Gift
Translated by Stephen E. Lewis

·